Gluck and the birth
of modern Opera

PATRICIA HOWARD

Gluck and the birth of modern Opera

Barrie and Rockliff
London

© 1963 *by Patricia Howard*
First published 1963 by
Barrie and Rockliff (Barrie Books Ltd)
2 Clement's Inn, London WC2
Printed in Great Britain by
W. & J. Mackay and Co Ltd
Fair Row, Chatham, Kent

Contents

Gluck and the birth
of modern Opera

Chapter one

Gluck and the Reform of Opera

THE personality of any artist who has become famous as a reformer arouses considerable interest. Gluck has, however, a tendency to infuriate reform-conscious historians by a number of surprising turns of character: he was apparently unaware of any need for the reform of opera until middle age, and then acted upon his principles only when prodded on to the rails by his librettists; furthermore, he disconcerted his admirers by reverting to his earlier style at frequent intervals – the style that he (even if through the pen of the librettists) denounced most vigorously in the reform opera prefaces; and finally he offended against all instinctively held values by culminating his career with a compara-tive failure.

Gluck was forty-eight when *Orfeo ed Euridice* was first produced. Between that year and his death at seventy-three, he wrote six more reform operas and at least seven retrogressions to his earlier style. This is the problem facing any attempted penetration of Gluck's character: in what light did Gluck himself view his work in general and his reform in particular – in what light could he view it – to produce such a rich but illogical succession of operas? The biography of any artist requires some relationship to be observed between 'life' and 'works', between the character of the man, formed by race, family, and historical environ-ment, and the products of the composer, influenced by education and contact with other musicians. Gluck's musical achievements are unusual. His enormous success as a conventional composer did not prevent him from expecting/ perhaps an unreasonable degree of acclaim/ for his *admiration* reformed works. As a great composer, fully conscious of his own powers up to their not inconsiderable limits, Gluck provides a fascinating study of the inter-reaction of opportunity and inclination.

Gluck's childhood is badly documented and offers fertile ground for suppositions and assumptions. We can now be certain that he was born on 2nd July 1714 at Erasbach in the Upper Palatinate, into a family of foresters and huntsmen with no known musical ancestors. But until 1732, when he went to Prague, presumably (and only presumably) to the university, there are few facts regarding his education and upbringing which cannot be contested. The salient fact that emerges is that Gluck was no prodigy, and in his early life excited no unusual interest in high places. His first position in 1736 took him to Vienna as a chamber musician, singer, and instrumentalist, to the Lobkowitz household, in which service his father was now head forester. There is no evidence of composition at this stage – Gluck was simply serving the conventional apprenticeship of any domestic performer. It did bring about, however, Gluck's first contact with Vienna.

Vienna was to be important to Gluck, and in this first and brief visit he must have come into contact with much of its artistic character. Musically, it was an Italian city with Italian composers and singers taking first place in Church and Court performances. Fux and Caldara reigned respectively in these main centres of musical life. But Vienna was drawing to the end of an epoch; 1736 was the year of Caldara's death, signifying the breaking of the last link with the Baroque era. Caldara's last operas, which Gluck probably heard that year, were splendid but backward-looking works. The contrapuntal textures of his arias and lengthy choruses were already rejected in the modern style of Hasse and of Pergolesi, the latter also dying tragically early in this same year. Hasse represents the new operatic ideal. He was the perfect musical counterpart of the recently appointed Imperial Court Poet, Pietro Metastasio. The new form of opera had been introduced by Metastasio's predecessor, Apostolo Zeno, and consisted of a rationalization of the excesses of seventeenth-century opera. Mythological subjects in particular were abandoned because of the sprawling, inconsistent matter of their plots. Historical plots succeeded them, and these were reconstructed in the light of the courtly code and popular virtues of the day. Universal clemency, magnanimity, and a heart which could be overruled by the mind seem poor material for the essentially passionate art of serious opera. These, however, were the motive force of a dramatic style that had much in common with Corneille, except that tragedy was elegantly excluded from most of the action, and sincere emotions were presented 'once removed', not in the potential strength of metaphor but in the artificiality of simile. Hasse's opera – and all the new Italian music in Vienna – was the direct result of the Zeno-Metastasio libretto, the *alter ego* of the neatness and supremely polished euphony of their language. It was 'singers' opera' in that the vocal lines blossomed into fluent coloratura passages, and the accompaniment was usually reduced to the barest harmonic minimum, notwithstanding the delicacy and appropriateness of many of Hasse's orchestral textures. His prolific technique was proverbial. Dr Burney, meeting him nearly forty years later, asked for a list of all his operas, 'but he said he did not know it himself. However he promised to recollect the principal of them. . . .'

Metastasio was a curiously honest man to have aroused the enmity of Gluck's supporters in the 1750s. He seems to have lived the exemplary life of one of his own heroes, being virtuous and generous to a degree that must have excited jealousy, since it could not have provoked resentment. Metastasio's dramatic ideals were not, statement for statement, far removed from Gluck's own. In his letters to Jommelli and Hasse he frequently stresses the importance of the libretto and the necessary subservience of the music to the poetry, though this is the kind of remark that comes better from the musician than the poet. Metastasio criticized Jommelli's fully orchestrated accompaniments, and the overdisplayed virtuosity of the singers. But his own texts, with leisurely, balanced dialogues and innumerable 'metaphor arias', invited just those abuses of the dramatic that Gluck more actively sought to quell. Metastasian opera was, however, nearly perfect for the composers and audiences of the time, and his genius was appreciated and duly rewarded – 'counted among the greatest glories of her reign' by Maria Theresa, who may well have admired him equally for his irreproachable character as for the steady production of libretti set countless times by the composers of the day.

Again, a single comment from Burney spotlights a wholly characteristic attitude, both of Metastasio and of his century: '[Metastasio] thinks that Milton's *Paradise Lost* cannot be a perfect poem because it is in blank verse.' He was one of the last examples of the 'isolated' librettist, producing his works without collaboration or contact with the composer who was to set them. This very fact was repugnant to the reform librettists, who took themselves and their work as seriously as Romantic artists, and who, by establishing so intimate a link with their chosen

composer, claimed, uncontradicted, the credit for all that was good in
the reform operas. By ending the career of the isolated librettist they
contributed to an important ideal of the nineteenth century, the uniqueness of a work of art – a concept meaningless in Metastasio's artistic
world. Vienna in 1736 was already presaging a new era. It was the year
of the marriage of Maria Theresa, and her accession four years later
brought the shock of war, austerity, and temporary artistic stagnation.
But by this time Gluck was in Milan, serving his long Italian apprenticeship, choosing Metastasio as his first librettist, and the style of Hasse as a
model of the perfection of the singer's art towards which he was aiming.

Gluck went to Milan in 1737 under the aegis of Prince Melzi and
remained there eight years. It was for Milan and for the neighbouring
towns of Crema and Turin that Gluck wrote seven of his first ten operas,
the remaining three being performed in Venice. There are four years of
silence before the first opera, *Artaserse*, was produced in December 1741,
and the subsequent works from this earliest period followed increasingly
rapidly as Gluck's success grew. Milan was an ancient town with a
diminishing population. Its musical life, as with so many small Italian
towns with a reasonably numerous aristocracy, centred on the opera.
Lalande's *Voyage en Italie* gives a near-contemporary description of it.
Lalande seems to have been impressed by the size of the stage in comparison, perhaps, with the Paris Opéra, the target of much adverse
criticism at this period; also with the opulence of the box accommoda-
tion 'in which people here pass a quarter of their lives'. In spite of the
restaurants and gaming tables, it provided a good opportunity for young
composers, with daily performances and regular, if inattentive, audiences. Sammartini (his teacher), Lampugnani, and Leonardo Leo were
the composers with whom Gluck came chiefly into contact. Conformity
was certainly Gluck's aim in this formative period. Simplicity and energy
are already apparent in these early works, the result of his characteristically straightforward attitude to opera – Gluck never in his life wrote
lengthy ritornelli or vocal coloratura to the extent that was normal in
Hasse and Jommelli – and it must have been this inborn simplicity of
approach, completely innocent of reformatory motives, that attracted
attention to the very minor talent at this stage displayed.

For Gluck attracted at least enough attention to be invited to con-
tribute to two collaborative operas: in 1743 he wrote the first act for
Lampugnani's *Arsace* and in the following year contributed to a pastiche
La Finta Schiava, Gluck's first comic opera, in company with Maccari,

Vinci, and again Lampugnani. The pastiche method may be said to be typical of Gluck throughout his life – at least, material from this Milan period recurs right through into the reform period, with no inconsistency. This was common enough practice among eighteenth-century composers, particularly opera composers, but is not to be expected from a musician whose fame rests on his revolutionary change of style in middle age!

Gluck went to Milan with no extant compositions to his credit, and left it a fully-fledged opera composer. Circumstances had made him an Italian musician: it would indeed have been difficult for them to have directed him elsewhere at this stage. In 1745 he moved to another centre of Italian opera: he accompanied Prince Lobkowitz, still officially his patron, to London, to reopen the Italian opera at the Haymarket, with *La Caduta dei Giganti*, a pastiche work of which only one number of the small collection that has come down to us was newly composed for the occasion. London in the winter of 1745–6 provided little action for Gluck. His two operas, *La Caduta* and *Artamene*, had no success in a capital that was expressing a certain hostility to things Catholic (and therefore things Italian) subsequent to the defeated Jacobite rebellion. It did provide, however, a most important contact. In meeting Handel, sharing a concert with him, and receiving, if not accepting, his criticism and advice, Gluck came into personal contact with the finest musician who had yet crossed his path. He retained a profound admiration for Handel throughout his life, though he never apparently imitated the musical values of the older composer. In the two legendary remarks of Handel to Gluck at this time we may choose to find the answer to the progress of Gluck's whole operatic career; alternatively they may have merely been Handel's guess; taken together they make a shrewd cause-and-effect summary of Gluck's limitations: first, the comment that Gluck knew no counterpoint, second, the advice to take less trouble for English audiences. The lives of the two composers are full of interesting contrasts. Gluck found small-scale success early in life, and was rarely out of pocket after a daring operatic venture; Handel had had to fight for every success he gained, and financial difficulties dogged the productions of most of his operas and all but his last oratorios.

Burney, eager to claim an active part for England in the shaping of Gluck's career, is enthusiastic concerning both Gluck's reception in London in this year and the effect of it and of Handel's advice on his later search for 'plainness and simplicity'. But we need not take Burney's engaging enthusiasms too seriously. London was no milestone for Gluck at this stage in his career. It was important only as the first stage in an arduous period of five years during which he travelled through Europe as a conductor of an Italian opera company, composing occasional works for the festivities of various royal houses: *Le Nozze d'Ercole e d'Ebe* for the double marriages between Bavaria and Saxony in 1747, *Semiramide Riconosciuta* for Maria Theresa's birthday in 1748, and *La Contesa de' Numi* for the birth of an heir to the throne of Denmark in 1749.

The year 1750 was the year of Gluck's marriage, bringing with it financial independence and a new vista of ambitions. From this year till the end of his life, Gluck's most constant home was Vienna. This alone may have had a stabilizing effect on him; a reputation had to be established in contrast with the string of mild and transient successes across Europe. Certainly monetary security would have had its effect on such an intensely practical mind as Gluck's. Very shortly we find signs of a new independence in his attitude to his commissions. In 1752 the already 'famoso Kluk' was invited to contribute a score to the festivities on the name day of Charles III of Naples. Gluck refused the libretto offered him – *Arsace*, part of which he had already composed in 1743 – and insisted on Metastasio's *La Clemenza di Tito*, which he had recently come across and conducted in Hasse's version during his touring period. Thus Metastasio and Hasse were still much to the fore in Gluck's artistic viewpoint. However, this setting marks Gluck's first important work in what might be called the middle period, or first maturity, of his career. The music is the first he wrote that could truly be called individual. The people of Naples found it learned and difficult – it certainly contains some of Gluck's most contrapuntal music – but were wooed to delighted acclamation by the performance of the celebrated castrato Caffarelli. One of Caffarelli's most important arias in *La Clemenza* was to reappear as 'O malheureuse Iphigénie' in *Iphigénie en Tauride*, an aria which one immediately feels to be of the reform in its utter simplicity, and which aroused enough controversy among Neapolitan scholars to give Gluck fair warning for the future.

Gluck's position in Vienna was consolidated two years later when he was made Kapellmeister. From this year, 1754, began the pressure from outside; first from Count Durazzo, the Court Intendant, and later from Calzabigi, the adventurer-poet, beginning as an anti-Metastasio clique and ending with the reform of opera. *La Clemenza* is the only indication we have of any leanings Gluck may have felt towards reform before his engagement by the trouble-making Count. It provides slender grounds indeed, for in spite of Caffarelli's 'Se mai senti spirarti nel volto', it was on a more archaic plan than even the festival operas and the Milan group that preceded it. Although Gluck had from his earliest operas shown a tendency to simple means and inconspicuous technique, there is no single indication that he was dissatisfied with the opera his contemporaries were producing, or that he wished to dissociate himself from them. And yet by the time the prefaces to the reform operas were written he was working under the influence of no vague theories of neo-classical renaissance that might have been suggested to him by the poets Durazzo and Calzabigi, but to precise and almost technical specifications for the reform. This fact seems to make less probable the generally held view that the prefaces were the work of Calzabigi – at least the contents must have been stringently drawn up by Gluck himself. And in examining the period of the fifties, during which the crucial development was to take place, Gluck's innate potentialities and the influence of his colleagues become of the greatest importance.

Gluck's compositions in the decade that separates *La Clemenza* from *Orfeo* are the usual mixture of the significant and the trivial. *Le Cinesi* (1754) was a brief Metastasian comedy, and an uncommon example of Gluck's non-serious style; it was his first comic opera since the pastiche *La Finta Schiava*. The most interesting number is the first, a fully orchestrated recitative and aria in parody of the style of a tragic aria. *La Danza* in the following year was an even slighter pastoral scena, more in the nature of a cantata, again to a text by Metastasio. This was followed in the same year by *L'Innocenza Giustificata*, from which point many critics have dated the reform. The libretto is, significantly, Metastasian aria texts with Durazzo's own recitatives. Gluck's music reflects the duality of authorship – a number of the arias might have been written at any date in Gluck's life, one of the most impressive, in fact, being a new version of an aria from *Artamene*, ten years earlier. The scenes and choruses are much newer in approach, and reflect the stimulating guidance of Durazzo. With *Antigono*, written for Rome in 1756, Gluck reverts to a complete Metastasio text and the style of his earliest period, which again is copiously referred to. *Il Rè Pastore* dates from the December of the same year: another occasional opera, for the birthday celebrations of Francis I. This is a little-known work containing the same melodic richness and maturity found in *La Clemenza di Tito*, certainly Gluck's most important opera between *L'Innocenza Giustificata* and *Orfeo ed Euridice*. It was followed by the series of French comic operas of varying degrees of sophistication, and the slight though graceful wedding serenata *Tetide*, produced in 1760.

Gluck's relations, artistic and personal, with Metastasio during this period seem impossible to establish. He had, by 1762, set at least a dozen of Metastasio's texts, and was to set three more. Calzabigi later wrote that Gluck's cast of mind was contrary in every way to that of the Imperial Court Poet: so it appears from *Orfeo* onwards, but what evidence exists of this before Calzabigi came on the scene? Durazzo chose to champion Gluck against Metastasio, but there seem few grounds to justify this choice in 1755. Calzabigi, again, stresses that he first wrote his poem, *Orfeo*, and then 'chose Gluck' to compose it. We might well ask why. But among the many doubts that perhaps inevitably surround the conception of the reform, it is at least clear that the combination of Calzabigi and Gluck produced a brief series of utterly new masterpieces; and that Gluck continued to develop his concept of opera after he discarded Calzabigi; while, apart from *Orfeo*, *Alceste*, and *Paride ed Elena*, what little remains of Calzabigi's work lies virtually forgotten in settings by infinitely lesser composers.

Similarly there can be no doubt that the first moment of the collaboration resulted in the reform. *Orfeo* is so unequal a work that the temptation exists to group it with *L'Innocenza*, and perhaps even with *La Clemenza*, as a tentative experiment before the more finished, more continuous genius of *Alceste*. The overture of *Orfeo*, for example, is as bad as anything Gluck ever wrote – a sign perhaps that the reformatory awakening came first from the librettist rather than from the composer. Then, the last act is bad in the poem and disappointing in the opera. But the material between these sections speaks in a new language that Gluck had not tried out before in even the best moments in his earlier work. And how much of this he owed to Calzabigi! The French influence in the construction of the first act is undeniable, and was the result of Calzabigi's fairly extensive knowledge of the French stage. More surprising is the style which Gluck brings to complete it: quite unlike anything he had written before and, at least in the opening chorus number, distinctly related to Rameau, whose music Gluck may have heard on his way to London in 1745, though he had almost certainly not had the chance of hearing it since. It is possible that on seeing such a chorus-weighted score as Calzabigi had produced, Gluck was able to recall the tableaux movements of *tragédie lyrique*, though more likely that any connexion between Gluck and France at this moment was mere coincidence. Certainly the air that follows the opening chorus movement and the working out of the second act are pure Gluck: his personal style appearing for the first time in one of the brightest highlights of eighteenth-century opera.

The achievements of *Orfeo* were not those that could be ignored, and yet Gluck proceeded to ignore them for five years, showing either disappointment at the rather slowly won acclaim for *Orfeo*, or good business sense in the acceptance of the commissions which gave occasion for most of the operas before *Alceste*. Most probably the libretti he was offered were incapable of awakening in him 'that enthusiasm without which the production of all works of art is feeble and lifeless', as he wrote in 1781. Three Metastasio poems are among the commissions; *Il Trionfo di Clelia* for the new theatre in Bologna, *Il Parnasso Confuso* for Schönbrunn for the marriage of Joseph II to Maria Josepha, and *La Corona*, unperformed in Gluck's lifetime, since the Emperor never lived to celebrate the birthday for which it was composed. The last comic opera, *La Rencontre Imprévue*, finished off the sequence begun six years earlier, and apart from two ballet-pantomimes and a festive cantata *Il Prologo*, the only other composition from this period is the problematic *Telemacco*.

The first knowledge we have of this opera is in 1765, in spite of earlier criticism assigning it to 1750. It is undoubtedly a difficult work to date. Were it assumed to be pre-*Orfeo* it would stand with *La Clemenza* and *L'Innocenza* as one of Gluck's most forceful and dramatic though unequal pre-reform experiments. Coming after *Orfeo*, as there seems no reason to doubt, it must to some extent be associated with *Clelia*, *Il Parnasso* and the others, as a somewhat disappointing opera – though its good qualities, particularly among the arias, remain, of course, good. A feature that links it in an interesting manner with one of the ballets attributed to this year, *Semiramide*, is that much of the material in both these works recurs in the Paris operas. In *Telemacco* it is a matter of a couple of arias and an accompanied recitative, but in *Semiramide* the odd little fragments that turn up in the *Iphigénies* are persuasive evidence that much of Gluck's self-borrowings were unconscious: it is hard to believe that such an experienced composer would search a small ballet score written some fourteen years earlier to find a suitable figure to insert in the accompanied recitative of the *dea ex machina* in *Iphigénie en Tauride*, though it is highly probable that Gluck remembered an effectively danced ballet number which he re-used for his furies' chorus in the same opera.

Alceste was written and produced in 1767, and in this opera Gluck consolidates the new manner of *Orfeo*, this time continuously from over-ture to final chorus. *Alceste* lacks the overwhelming simplicity of *Orfeo*. There is more incident, if not action. There are more minor characters. And, in spite of the immense importance of the chorus in this opera, a more traditional distribution of aria and recitative, with the resultant wider range of styles, is found. Perhaps because of this the opera was more immediately successful than *Orfeo*. It was certainly more important to Gluck than *Orfeo*, for it was published two years later, with the famous preface which made it both impossible to have any more 'lapses' and important to make some progress in the reform. In fact, it put Gluck in the position of a nineteenth-century symphonic writer who realizes, surely with regret, that he can no longer compose in sets of six comple-mentary and similar works, but must create something both new and unique.

After *Alceste* Gluck produced no new opera for more than eighteen months. It was at this point that he formally adopted his ten-year-old niece, Marianne, whose singing tuition and musical education occupied him exclusively for a while. (Burney recounts that Gluck 'in a precipi-tate fit of despair' later entrusted her tuition to the famous castrato Millico, and the resultant precociously accomplished girl entertained him most impressively with arias from *Alceste* and others by various com-posers, including Traetta.) The only triviality which breaks the three-year gap between *Alceste* and *Paride* is a curious occasional festival opera for the marriage of one of Maria Theresa's daughters at Parma. *Le Feste d'Apollo*, 1769, consists of three acts plus a prologue on various themes of conjugality, including a one-act version of *Orfeo*. Much of the music was borrowed from previous recent operas, and it constituted no very sig-nificant departure from practice for Gluck, who was, after all, employed to produce such occasional music and quite possibly considered such commissions, accompanied as they were by the most unexciting libretti, as in a sphere quite removed from his serious operatic work.

Paride ed Elena was the third reform opera, and was both produced and published towards the end of 1770. *Paride*, taken with *Orfeo* and *Alceste*, shows the full scope of Calzabigi's imagination in the creation of three such different works. The similarities between *Paride* and *Orfeo* are numerous and will be discussed fully in the appropriate chapters, but far more important to Gluck were the differences: the third completely new world of emotions was laid before him and was matched in his setting by an individuality of approach of which one tends to deny the existence in eighteenth-century *opera seria*. As with *Alceste*, Calzabigi had considerable plot reconstruction to effect. *Orfeo* is damaged by a contrived 'happy ending' irrelevant to the nature of the work. *Alceste* ends properly – on a note of wonder and speculation rather than uninhibited joy. *Paride* has a dark ending – like *Alceste* it is immediately reconciled, but bodes uncertainty for the future.

Gluck composed the new opera with complete seriousness. It was a magnificent opportunity to extend reform propaganda: to show extreme beauty of melody (and how very beautiful Paris' songs in the first act are!) as appropriate for one character, and to reject it in a style of great vigour and power for the opposite protagonist. The weakest aspect of the opera is the difficulty of retaining this clear-cut characterization at the point where the lovers are finally reconciled: Gluck never again attempts such extremes of style. But it is upon this racial and personal stylistic dichotomy that the opera depends, and the success of Gluck's theories, which was not reflected in the immediate demand for this opera, was one which was to play an important, if more subtle, part in the subsequent reform operas.

As we should expect, the frequency of the operas declines with their originality, and four years passed before *Iphigénie en Aulide* produced instant acclaim and controversy in Paris. From external events, we can deduce that Gluck had in this interval concerned himself with the problems of other languages and their appropriateness to music. His friendship with Klopstock dates from this period, and several of the odes were probably composed in the early 1770s. His début in French serious opera was the next step. A French opera for Paris – and two years of preparation before *Iphigénie* could be successfully produced in 1774.

The libretto was completed in 1772, and the opera composed that year. In August, Du Roullet, the new librettist, writes of repeated hearings of the music. And Burney's visit to Vienna in September substantiates this, providing one of the few indications we have of Gluck's methods of composition: '[Gluck] was so good humoured as to perform almost his whole opera of *Alceste*; many admirable things in a still later opera of his called *Paride ed Elena*; and in a French opera, from Racine's *Iphigénie* which he has just composed. This last, though he had not as yet committed a note of it to paper, was so well digested in his head, and his retention is so wonderful, that he sung it nearly from the beginning to the end with as much readiness as if he had a fair score before him.' But

Paris was a hotbed of artistic intrigues and partisanship and the way had to be prepared to disarm as many potential enemies as possible. The Opéra was suffering the lack of a good serious opera composer to follow Rameau. After the notorious *guerre des bouffons* that followed the invasion of Paris by the Italian *opera buffa* in the early 1750s, national pride and national shame had been at stake. Jean-Jacques Rousseau was the chief supporter of Italian opera and spared no efforts to decry the French language as unmusical, and French opera as a barren absurdity. Other leaders of artistic thought, among the Encyclopaedists, were equally consistent supporters of *opera buffa*, although they also favoured the creation of a new serious opera, based on the Italian conventions. A very significant fact arising from this situation is that the theorists who clamoured most vehemently for or against various kinds of opera never opened their mouths on the subject of instrumental music, which was plentiful and quite international in Paris. This is as much a comment on the nature of opera as on these critics: opera has always provided for the attention of the non-musician by the very constitution of the whole form. But the many months of soothing, wooing negotiations with the Opéra directors and the public that occupied Gluck and Du Roullet in the years between composition and performance were a reflection on Paris itself, and its uniquely turbulent climate of thought.

It is obvious that Du Roullet's persistent tact and caution were of immense value in preparing the way for the first performance. Himself a minor diplomat of the French embassy in Vienna, he planned the reception of the work as a delicate treaty of peace. For his own protection, Du Roullet claimed merely to have converted Racine's drama into an opera, and avoided criticism (of his share in the opera) by disclaiming praise for originality. His first move was an open letter to D'Auvergne, a director of the Opéra, published in the *Mercure de France* in October 1772, praising Gluck's musical genius, and explaining the economic advantages of the opera. ('I do not think any one has ever produced a new opera requiring less expenditure to achieve so imposing an effect. . . . M. Glouch, very disinterested by nature, asks only the amount fixed by the management for the composers of new operas.') This was followed up in the subsequent February by Gluck's letter to the editor of the *Mercure*, in which he attributes the entire moving spirit of the reform to Calzabigi, and pays an expedient compliment to Rousseau enabling him to link their names without any more material grounds than a projected collaboration which was never effected. D'Auvergne's reception of this correspondence and the first act of the score was scarcely enthusiastic, though his reply was guarded and courteous enough to preserve the tone of these diplomatic negotiations: Gluck's opera was accepted only on condition that he produced five others to follow it, which lucrative though arduous commission he seems to have accepted instantly, and rehearsals – some of the most famous and troublesome rehearsals in the history of opera – were in progress by the autumn.

It was fortunate that during these tentative and time-wasting exchanges Gluck had personally ensured the protection of his former singing pupil, the Dauphine Marie Antoinette. Her support could hardly have been won on the grounds of *Iphigénie's* artistic merit, for in the later amateur theatricals at Versailles there is no evidence that Marie Antoinette took any interest in important operatic developments of her age. The royal patronage more likely arose from injunctions from her mother, and from the claims of a longstanding friendship with her fellow countryman whose forthright and uncompromising conduct during the rehearsals ('I shall go to the Queen and tell her it is impossible to produce my opera. Then I shall get into my coach and make straight for Vienna!') seemed refreshing after the confining conduct of the Court. The success of the first night was very largely due to the Dauphine; the performance was to have been given on 13th April, but owing to the illness of the singer who was to play Achilles, Gluck postponed the performance till the 19th. Only the public example of Marie Antoinette achieved a full house after the cancelled earlier arrangements. Naïvely, however, she expressed astonishment that controversy should follow the performance, in spite of her own prominently voiced approval!

Gluck followed *Iphigénie* with new versions of *Orfeo* and *Alceste* and also of the two *opéras-comiques*, *L'Arbre Enchanté* and *La Cythère Assiégée*. None of these works did much to establish his fame in Paris, and the destruction of *Roland* was perhaps what the meddling, sensation-seeking Opéra management deserved. Gluck's lucrative and distinguished appointment as Imperial Court Composer in Vienna – the exact definition of his earlier appointment under Durazzo was never clarified, and was the subject of some dispute – commenced on 18th October 1774, and gave Gluck a feeling of independence and due appreciation of his talents that contrasted sharply with his treatment in Paris. He is certainly very offhand and dictatorial with regard to offering *Armide* for performance at the Opéra: 'I must be given at least two months after I arrive at Paris, to train my actors and actresses; I must have complete authority to require as many rehearsals as I shall think necessary; there will be no understudies and another opera shall be held in readiness in case one of the actors or actresses were indisposed. These are my conditions without which I shall keep *Armide* for my own pleasure. I have fashioned the music in such a way that it will not quickly age.' Gluck arrived in Paris in May 1777. Rehearsals began in July and the first performance took place towards the end of September.

Armide was a strange and unpredictable moment in the reform. Gluck has been shown to have been very heavily dependent upon his librettists if he were to write anything significant. Yet for *Armide* he took a libretto by Quinault – by Lully's gifted poet. Being nearly a hundred years old, this poem was anything but suited to the modern Gluck. He may have chosen Quinault as a compliment, as a further step in the tactful persuasion which we have seen enacted between composer and management in this hard-fought conquest of Parisian opera. It is more likely, though, that Gluck had been genuinely attracted by the other Quinault work he had met – the unrevised poem of *Roland*, recently rejected – and found in the character of Armida herself scope for the portrayal of another splendid 'heroine' in the tradition of Alcestis, Helen, and Iphigenia.

The last two reform operas were written virtually simultaneously during 1778, and were accepted from the librettists Guillard and Von Tschudi. Both were performed the following year. Guillard's poem, *Iphigénie en Tauride*, provided Gluck with the necessary 'enthusiasm' to produce his finest opera and won him, justly, his greatest acclaim in Paris. It was undoubtedly the climax of the reform and many aspects of the earlier operas can be found perfected in it: the action presentation of the furies, the solemnity of sacrificial ritual, racial characterization and, newest and most accomplished for Gluck, the compelling portrayal of the intimate relationships between sister, brother, and friend that makes it one of the few great operas lacking the motivation of erotic passion.

Echo et Narcisse was a vastly less fortunate choice. Von Tschudi was an amateur and there is no evidence of any previous libretto from his pen. The opera was to be another experiment for Gluck, just as *Orfeo* and *Armide* had been experiments: the whole framework of the opera was new, and the creation of living characters from the shadowy figures of mythology was a challenge to both poet and composer and one to which neither fully responded. It is an interesting comment on Gluck's character that, after so late and stolidly conventional a start to his career, at the age of sixty-four he was preparing to risk his reputation in a completely fresh approach to operatic forms. The new qualities in *Echo* – the extremely rich orchestration and the refined, more detailed expression of the vocal line – passed unnoticed in the face of the poor dramatic construction of the whole. To the end of his life Gluck never ceased to express bitterness on the subject of the reception of his last opera. He died in Vienna eight years later.

It is difficult to reconstruct any complete picture of Gluck's character from his actions and writings, much less from his music. It is easy enough to trace the symptoms of the competent professional, from the earliest period learning to write operas that would please, not hesitating to repeat successful numbers in subsequent works, and, lacking the equipment of the performer virtuoso, exploiting the 'curious as well as the lovers of music' by his performances on the glass harmonica. It is also possible to trace a growing independence of thought coinciding with increasing material security. Showing no visible revulsion against Metastasio, Gluck allowed himself to be used in the movement to dethrone the Court Poet, while later refusing to take part in a mere journalist-created trial of strength with a composer he had no cause to despise. There is no obvious explanation for the brevity of his friendship with Calzabigi. The variety among the first three reform operas hardly suggests that boredom or dissatisfaction drove Gluck to Paris. Certainly some strong attraction, other than his contract, held him there and gave him the incentive to fight so determinedly for acknowledgement and success.

These contradictions and inconsistencies prevent a definitive assessment of what the reform meant to Gluck. Gluck's part in the reform, on the other hand, is a more concrete matter and is contained in the seven – perhaps six – masterpieces of his maturity, which have few predecessors in music, though many in theory, and fewer successors. Lack of followers had disturbed him from the beginning of the reform – notably in the *Paride* preface he complains of the 'paths already opened up' which were ignored by others. It is one sure quality that stamps him as being typical of his own century – this desire for others to do what he has done, rather than seeking or at least rejoicing in the uniqueness of the Romantic artist's creation. And only by seeing Gluck against the eighteenth century, and the reform as part of a movement that occupied the whole of it, can we appreciate the unexaggerated importance of his place in the history of opera, and the place of opera in the history of music.

Chapter two

The Seeds of Reform

OPERA, by the very nature of its origins, has invited the participation of theorists in shaping its history. The dilettante and professional have equally claimed this right of criticism accorded to no other musical form. The entirely new developments which took place in the sonata and the symphony in the early nineteenth century, which appear to us today to be considerably more revolutionary than those developments in eighteenth-century opera achieved by Gluck, were not preceded by prefaces or manifestoes, the only literature associated with them being the explanatory programmes or titles. No one thought to call them reformed. No one thought to praise or parody in any but the normal channels of musical criticism. That opera has laid itself open to this, however, is due in part to the variety of artistic causes involved; the history of opera consists of the exploitation of one of these at the expense of the others, with inevitable reaction and reversal. Another reason for its vulnerability is the close connexion between opera and the societies in which it has variously flourished – societies which are reflected by all the art works of their time, but nowhere more faithfully nor perhaps more eccentrically than in opera.

Criticism may take the form of musical parody: in this way the idea of comic opera was evolved, transplanted, and cultivated throughout Europe in the eighteenth century, bearing fruit in instrumental music with far wider consequences than the original act of parody could have foreseen. More often, however, discontent was not expressed so constructively. Literary satire and criticism of the conventional opera appeared continuously throughout the first half of the century. In spite of the violence with which much of this was expressed, it is difficult to estimate its influence on librettists and composers, for those who were aware of the inadequacies of the stage conventions published their own manifestoes – Noverre's *Lettres sur la dance* and Gluck's prefaces, documents composed after the fact, after the first reform works had been written and performed. Beside these, the ridicule of less active participants, in articles by personalities as different as Addison and Rousseau, had smaller impact, because it was generally unrealistic, demanding little compromise with tradition, ignoring the continuity which underlies all development of style even through a period of reform: the approach was almost wholly destructive.

These writings are important, however, in that they show the climate of thought in which the active reformers worked. The fact that these reformers not only had many of the most eloquent critics on their side, but had also been urged to express dissatisfaction with the contemporary opera for many years before they came to take action, serves to show the reform in the light of a foreseeable development, long expected by those who were aware of the situation.

There is a remarkable similarity in the targets at which the reformers, both composers and theorists, aimed. One of the earliest comprehensive attacks is Benedetto Marcello's satire *Il Teatro alla moda*, published about 1720. This is written in the form of 'useful and necessary recommendations to Poets, Composers of music, Singers of either sex, Impresarios, Musicians, Designers and painters of sets, Costumers, Attendants, Supernumaries, Prompters, Copyists, Protectors and Mothers of lady singers and other persons concerned with the theatre'. The style is direct and amusing, the subject-matter a malicious exaggeration of the so-called corruption of Italian opera – 'so-called' because it is important to realize throughout this splendid satire that the criticism came about simply because of differing interpretations of the word 'drama'. A Handelian aria and a stage 'machine' are no less incipiently dramatic than a Gluckian scene continuously composed in accompanied recitative, with an acting chorus. But with opera, of all forms of music the most closely concerned with fashion and with the fashionable world closely concerned with opera, absolute values are out of the question.

Il Teatro is perceptive in many of its details, however, criticizing above all the subservience of every aspect of opera to the singer's whim, of rational narrative to the stereotyped succession of moods, of expression to the brilliance of coloratura on unimportant words – in short, of the

dramatic to the peculiar form of aria then in vogue. Marcello wrote:
'Let [the composer] write arias throughout the opera which are alternately lively and pathetic, regardless of the words, nature or conduct of
the scene. If nouns e.g. padre, impero, amore, arena, regno, beltà, lena,
core, etc., or adverbs, e.g. no, senza, già, etc., occur in the arias, the
modern composer should write passage-work melismata upon them,
e.g. paaa . . . impeeee . . . amoooo . . . areee . . . reeee . . . bel-
tàaaa . . . lenaaa . . . etc.; nooo . . . seeee . . . giàaaa etc. The object is to get away from the old style which did not use melismata on
nouns or adverbs, but only on words expressing some passion.' Marcello
is sufficiently in advance of his time to criticize the free plagiarism of
arias from either the composer's own previous works, or from those of
others, and in connexion with this, the established techniques of aria
composition: the unison aria, for example, and the overlong and irrelevant ritornelli are attacked on the grounds of inappropriateness to the
drama. The fact that Marcello, in his own compositions, never attempted a reform of opera gives a certain lack of urgency to the work, though
it does not diminish its relevance to the reform movement.

Thirty years later the critics of opera had become more militant.
There is more that is constructive in Algarotti's essay, published in 1755,
closely preceding the manifestoes of Gluck and Noverre. It is an interesting link with the French operatic controversy, since Algarotti was
attached to Parma, the centre of French influence which left its mark on
Traetta's work there. Algarotti's attitude is essentially moderate and
reasonable, the argument of the essay being set out as a comparison
between opera and society which 'it is impossible to preserve from decay
and in the unimpaired enjoyment of constitutional vigour without
making it return from time to time to its original principles'. Algarotti
does indeed revert to the principles of the first operas, above all, their
homogeneity of style; and after making the inevitable plea for the
primacy of poem and poet, he suggests a levelling of musical interest:
added importance for the recitatives, and less isolation of the arias. This
criticism may well have arisen not only from the practice of Peri and
Caccini but from the continuity observed in French opera with which he
had made contact. Certainly Algarotti is very aware of the French
traditions. He specifically contrasts the irrelevance of the Italian diver-
timento with the appropriateness and unity at times found in the French
use of such interludes; and similarly he compares the importance
attached to acting in the two countries: in Italy the subject scarcely

coming into consideration, and in France precious interpretations of famous roles being handed down through overconservatism of both singer and public. Algarotti, however, finds his ideal of 'beautiful simplicity' – his language is often very close to that of the *Alceste* preface – in the influential *opera buffa*. For more constructive criticism of Italian serious opera we must examine Gluck's own viewpoint expressed in the prefaces to his reform operas.

With the preface to *Alceste*, published in 1769, the reform had been accomplished. The style is authoritative, and Gluck is obviously aware of his unique position. It is difficult indeed to realize when we read of the disfigurements which 'have made of the most splendid and most beautiful of spectacles, the most ridiculous and wearisome', that Gluck's own operatic history included so many of these 'ridiculous' and 'wearisome' works. So much for the inevitable change of character observable in one who has turned to attack rather than comply with conventions! The preface adds nothing new to the previous critical essays we have noted. It deals in turn with the domination of the singers, the proposal to restrict music to the office of servant to the drama, the lack of drama in the aria, the new function of the overture, and the continuity between aria and recitative to be brought about by the expressive use of the orchestra. It is difficult to assess the value of Gluck's tributes to Calzabigi. These are certainly recurrent throughout the collaboration, though they flow mostly from Calzabigi's own pen, both in the published letters and, if the authorship is indeed his, in the prefaces themselves.

New claims are made in the preface to *Paride ed Elena*, published in 1770 – the year of the performance – unlike *Orfeo* and *Alceste*, which had both to wait two years for publication, two years in which 'success justified my theories', as Gluck states in the *Alceste* preface. The main theme he discusses in the *Paride* preface is characterization in opera, a problem which had not previously appeared in criticism, apart from Algarotti's advocation of remote subjects and characters in opera, 'for who can be brought to think that the trillings of an air flow so justly from the mouth of a Julius Caesar or a Cato as from the lips of Venus or Apollo?' This recalls a rebuke made by Gluck to Vestris, the choreographer for *Armide*: 'If Tasso had wished to make Rinaldo a dancer, he would not have displayed him in the guise of a warrior.' The problem raised in *Paride* is, however, more specifically musical. Gluck claims to have differentiated between the nations of Phrygia and Sparta, even, when necessary, to the extent of sacrificing purely musical values: 'When

truth is sought, it must be varied in accordance with the subject we have
to work out, and the greatest beauties of melody and harmony would
become defects and imperfections if out of place.' Few musicians have
claimed this. The statement is a very personal one, and lies at the heart
of the reform. It was at the same time both criticism of the existing
Italian opera and defence against almost any possible criticism of
Gluck's own work. For judgement could not be made on Gluck's aims,
although it might be recognized that these aims produced a form of
opera singularly well suited to his limitations as an absolute musician.
Gluck's genius lay in the recognition of his own limitations, and in his
ability to turn these to such valuable purpose. Such principles are rarely
found in a musician – an important reason for Gluck's failure to found a
new school of opera.

A fact which was both of great help to Gluck in carrying out his
innovations, and also substantiates our impression of the reform as being
part of a natural artistic development rather than a *volte face* on the part
of one man, is the unrest and change which were felt in two parallel arts
at this time: the ballet and the libretto. Noverre's *Lettres sur la dance* have
already been mentioned. These were published in 1760, and record the
theories of Jommelli's collaborator in Stuttgart. In his contribution to the
reformed ballet Gluck collaborated with Angiolini, who was to some
extent a rival of Noverre, in that, although working towards the same
end, he disputed the originality of Noverre's theories and attributed
them to his predecessor as Viennese ballet master, Hilverding. It seems,
however, that Noverre was probably the first to make his innovations
public. He was a widely travelled man and his influences ranged from
the dramatic use of the dance in Rameau's operas to the expressive
mime of David Garrick.

His aims everywhere foreshadow the trends of the opera prefaces: the
terms 'beautiful simplicity' and 'imitation of nature' occur frequently.
And yet opera is still empty spectacle for him: 'L'opéra n'est fait que
pour les yeux et les oreilles; il est moins le spectacle du coeur et de la
raison, que celui de la variété et de l'amusement', and again: 'Fait il
une ouverture? Elle n'est point relative à l'action qui va se passer,
qu'importe après tout? N'est-il pas sûr de la réussite si elle fait grand
bruit?' These views emphasize the independence of the two reform
movements and the widespread dissatisfaction with the existing operatic
style. Noverre sought to replace the 'geometry of the dance' with pantomime. The fine technique of abstract dance was to give way to acting

and expression; the hindering costumes – the *paniers* and *tonnelets* of Racine and Rameau's stage – were to be replaced by simpler garments. Realism and simplicity were strongly advocated; the dancers should 'abandonner leur allure et prendre une âme', the music should be 'parlante et expressive'.

The irrelevance of the divertissement in French opera had long been criticized and one of Rameau's developments was to link this dance interlude more closely with the plot. The mixture of the Oriental with the Classical had gone to ridiculous lengths in his day, giving fantastic and highly coloured opportunities for the ballet. Critics soon recognized the skill of Rameau's chief librettist, Cahusac, in making the dance more relevant and therefore more dramatic. Rameau's best operas are probably *Dardanus* and *Castor et Pollux*. In both of these we find the ballet *entrées* introduced with pleasing continuity. In the second act of *Castor*, for example, an *entrée* occurs where Hébé and the *Plaisirs célestes* try to hinder Pollux from descending into the underworld. The libretto gives the programme of the dance: 'Hébé danse à la tête des Plaisirs célestes, tenant dans leurs mains des guirlandes de fleurs dont ils veulent enchaîner Pollux.' Although this was probably danced in the very geometric figures Noverre denounced, at least it has a dramatic tension derived from the plot. Sometimes the dance became the centre of the action. In *Zoroastre*, for example, 'les esprits infernaux, conduits par la Haine et le Désespoir, accourent à la voix de la Vengeance; elle se place au pied de l'autel; les démons armés de serpents et de poignards, font contre la statue de Zoroastre les plus redoutables conjurations . . . un tourbillon de flammes sort de l'autel et la statue disparaît.' These are the scenes which influenced and inspired Noverre, and gave him material for his new style of dancing. The passion, the simple tragedy, and the sharp characterization he required of his ballet plots are all to be found in the interludes of Cahusac and Rameau.

The part played by the dance in the operas of Jommelli and Traetta arose from the influence both of the traditional French stage and of Noverre's new teaching. In both composers' works the dance is usually closely associated with the sung chorus, and the increased function of this component of opera was a significant aspect of the reform and will be discussed later: for example, the recurring chorus 'Della gran buccina' from the first act of Jommelli's *Fetonte*, and the extended scenes of dance and chorus portraying the furies in Traetta's *Iphigenia*.

The influence of all three composers upon Gluck is very apparent.

Gluck's reform ballet, *Don Juan*, has already been mentioned. It contains powerfully dramatic music throughout, and although some of the movements are more closely connected with traditional dance forms than the dances in the later operas (the perfectly characterized gavotte, danced by the aristocratic guests in Act II, for example), the ballet of the furies later reappears in the French version of *Orfeo*, when it is shown to be among the most dramatic musical utterances in the opera. It is interesting, incidentally, to find Gluck writing instrumental music on such a large time-scale; most of his instrumental music is dance music and it is in this context that his melodic invention is most severely exposed. In *Don Juan* Gluck comes off very well in this respect. The melodic grace, which is rarely a virtue in the operas, and which, indeed, we are inclined to overlook in Gluck's musical character in favour of the simple dramatic stroke or psychologically revealing recitative, can here be enjoyed for its own sake. It also contributes to the effective communication of the mood and scene: the almost waltz-like A major andante; the siciliano with which the Don serenades Donna Elvira in the first act, with its persuasive melancholy that may well have been learned from Handel, who used the same metre for love songs; and the 'local colour' of the fandango, which has attracted notice because of its resemblance to Mozart's in *Figaro*.

The ballet music in the reform operas is fully consistent with the trends in *Don Juan*. The dance and chorus play an important part in Gluck's most potent sphere of dramatic art – characterization. Gluck is always most effective when he is contrasting one nation with another: the musical dichotomy between the races of Phrygia and Sparta, for example, or Scythia and Greece, and the dramatic contrast between the Furies and the Blessed Spirits comes within the same technique. By the time he wrote the *ballet pantomime de terreur* in *Iphigénie en Tauride*, the complete absence of stylization or connexion with the traditional forms of Baroque dance music is indicative of the ballet's successful progress towards naturalism and drama. (EX. 1)

The part played by the librettists in creating an atmosphere and situation in which the reform of opera could be carried out is an interesting and important one. It has the same duality of circumstances as those surrounding Gluck. For him, as we have seen, both the climate of thought of his age and his own musical qualities – or, more relevantly, weaknesses – tended towards the kind of music we find in *Orfeo* and *Alceste*. The decline of the Metastasian libretto was foreseen by the same librettists who had ridiculed its too compliant composers, but this would probably have failed to bring about the almost complete neglect of Metastasio by future composers were it not for a very influential clique determined to oppose the Imperial Court Poet from motives both personal and artistic.

EX. I

The opposition was formed gradually. As we have said, the instigator was Count Durazzo, who made his first move by engaging Gluck in 1754. Significantly the first fruit of the alliance was the *festa teatrale, L'Innocenza Giustificata*, frequently considered as the starting-point for reform tendencies in Gluck's work. Against the recitative scenes by Durazzo, the Metastasian aria texts appear more than usually banal. (It would be quite in keeping with the little we know of Durazzo's character to suspect him of planning this contrast deliberately.) Germs of dramatic incidents in later operas can be found here; and the reform's avowed overthrow of music by drama is deftly symbolized when Valerius and Flavius hasten to interrupt Claudia's aria with the announcement of the miraculous climax.

Another move by Durazzo concerned the importation of *opéras-comiques* into Schönbrunn. At first the musically primitive originals were performed, and became fashionable light relief from Italian opera. Gluck's composed *opéras-comiques* date from 1758, with *L'Isle de Merlin* and *La Fausse Esclave*. These and the succeeding works gave the composer a chance to experiment in the simplest of melodic styles, in drama ranging from the mythological *La Cythère Assiégée* to the vividly colloquial *L'Ivrogne Corrigé*. This simplicity – at times economy amounting to parsimony – of melody reappears as an important aspect of the reform. Some of the arias in *Orfeo* exemplify this – an originally plebeian language exalted to serious opera.

When Calzabigi arrived in Vienna in 1761 the personalities of the reform were assembled. It is difficult to find the exact turning-point in Calzabigi's life that gave him reform tendencies. His early career as librettist showed his whole-hearted allegiance to Metastasio. This was maintained at least publicly as late as 1755, when he wrote as preface to the complete edition of Metastasio's works, in Paris, the *Dissertazione su le poesie drammatiche del Sig. Abate Pietro Metastasio*. Not that Calzabigi was incapable of hypocrisy! Together with Algarotti, Da Ponte, Goldoni, and many of the most interesting characters of the century, he was a widely travelled adventurer, a resourceful, worldly poet, who was perfectly able to compromise artistic ideals with expediency and advancement. Casanova writes admiringly of his more ingenious escapades and regards him as a rival in the brand of confidence trick in which the eighteenth century excelled. And so it seems impossible to deduce whether Calzabigi turned the antagonism of Durazzo and Gluck to his own use, or whether genuine and impersonal artistic convictions led him to guide Gluck towards the new operatic style. Whichever is true, his influence was undeniable and decisive in Gluck's career and the reform of opera.

And Calzabigi was continually protesting the importance of his contribution to the reform. He maintained to the last that he had selected Gluck as the fittest composer to set his poems, rather than that Durazzo had brought them together in their mutual interest. Gluck never offered any opposition to any claim by Calzabigi; 'it is to M. Calzabigi that the foremost merit belongs', he wrote some years after his break with his librettist; 'however much talent a composer has, he will never rise above mediocrity unless the poet is able to awaken in him that enthusiasm without which the production of all works of art is feeble and lifeless.' That Gluck's operas are not 'feeble and lifeless' when he rejects Calzabigi for Du Roullet in the first Paris operas serves to show both the enduring strength of Calzabigi's influence on Gluck and the changes which had meanwhile taken place in opera itself. In fact, it was probably Calzabigi who turned Gluck's thoughts towards French opera. All the innovations in the three operas on which they collaborated can ultimately be traced back to French opera; and earlier in his life, in the

Dissertazione, Calzabigi showed he was well aware of the possible effect of the brilliant ensemble that often characterized French productions, 'che dal coro numeroso, dal ballo, dalla scena maestrevolmente unita colla poesia e colla musica. . . .'

As we saw in *L'Innocenza Giustificata* the librettist's influence lies chiefly in two spheres of opera: the recitative, and the action – the division of incidents, the structure of the opera in all senses other than musical. In these the reform was achieved by the librettist and handed as an accomplished fact to the composer. Calzabigi was the first librettist to do this for Gluck, and, as far as we can see, the first to do it for any composer. Calzabigi's professed beliefs, and those that brought about the cardinal crux of the reform, were in the importance of incident on the stage rather than narration of incident: 'La parte principalissima della Tragedia essenda l'azione e non la declamazione' – a fitting precept for the self-styled creative power behind the revolutionary scene.

Chapter three

Reform Composers before Gluck

AND now we must pass from comment and theory to musical fact, for the reform of opera was prepared for in the works of a number of eighteenth-century composers, some of whom seem to anticipate Gluck's developments by accident, others by genuinely seeking a more dramatic expression of opera. Generally speaking, no composer before Gluck combined all the developments that were to appear in *Alceste*. Some introduced the all-important feeling for continuity and the new function of the chorus that went far in achieving this; others built up the recitative scena. And the vast majority of thinking composers were modifying the 'da capo' aria, both from boredom with the excessively lengthy form, and also under the influence of the songs from comic opera – *opera buffa*, *opéra-comique*, and *Singspiel*, as it appeared in the different countries.

The changes brought about in French opera during the century were the first signs of the coming reform. Rameau's influence on Gluck is probably the least direct of those under discussion. His relevance lies in the traditions he upheld, and those he founded for the opera in Paris. We know how deeply Gluck was affected by the Paris traditions, and that his last and finest operas were to break through the insularity which had previously segregated the French stage from the rest of European developments. But without the segregation, French opera would not have had anything new to contribute to the otherwise universal Italian style. It is, however, impossible to assess Rameau's innovations and to understand the hostility they evoked without being aware of the extreme conservatism that had grown up during the time of Lully – to such an extent that Rameau, writing nearly seventy years later, was criticized for breaking with the past! And yet at first glance his works seem to differ so slightly from Lully's that we might almost overlook the advancement. The Italian influence on Rameau is small, and is restricted to the frankly melodic *ariettes* which are usually found in the least dramatic part of the work, the divertissement. In these infrequent pieces Rameau displays the characteristics of a short Italian aria, isolated from the progress of the action by a brief ritornello, and differentiated from the mainly declamatory vocal line of the rest of the arias by a restrained coloratura. Every other aspect of Rameau's style is wholly French, and reappears thoroughly assimilated into the style of Gluck's maturest work.

The choruses are the greatest single feature of Rameau's operas, and it is these which make their most apparent mark on Gluck. The extended choral scene – 'Que tout gémisse' in *Castor et Pollux*, for example – was the exact mood that Gluck hit upon for the opening of *Orfeo*, and approaches also the monumental dignity of the prayer scenes in *Alceste* and the *Iphigénies*. Rameau's furies in the same opera make an interesting use of unison singing which lacks the force of the *Orfeo* furies only because Rameau had an older, less brutal concept of dramatic rhythm:

EX. 2

This chorus, mild as it seems beside Gluck's infernal scenes, gave rise to this interesting contemporary tribute from the French critic Chabanon: 'Jamais nous n'avons entendu ce passage sans éprouver ce frissonnement qui fait pointer les cheveux de la tête.' Also foreshadowing Gluck's practices, Rameau introduces short exclamations by the chorus, inevitably of the most effective nature. These are obviously uninteresting in musical content, written with the intention of leaving the singers free to act: 'à Lully il faut les chanteurs, à moi les acteurs', a comment which underlines the views in the *Alceste* preface, though it does not account for the stiff, unnatural chorus which Gluck found in rehearsal for *Iphigénie en Aulide*.

This dramatic continuity was to be Rameau's chief gift to Gluck. Besides the chorus fragments, short instrumental phrases link passages of recitative; these Gluck developed to accompany pregnant moments of decision, as in so many recitatives of Iphigenia in *Iphigénie en Tauride*. Rameau's recitative and arias are both tenser rhythmically than Lully's, and some of the harmonic experiments which occupied his research and theoretical writings can be felt – in a number of scenes in *Dardanus*, particularly. The recitative flows much more slowly than in Italian opera to make space for the ornaments and to make the time changes effective. Also the melodic intervals are generally larger than in Italian opera. One or two of Gluck's arias in the Paris operas show the influence of Rameau's small-scale declamatory airs. Rameau had no problem of the *da capo* form to contend with; he only used it in its simplest mid-seventeenth-century form, and in the more extended *ariettes*, previously mentioned. Gluck's debt to Rameau lies rather in the French composer's revitalizing of the tradition-bound style, stagnant since the death of Lully. Gluck ended the fiercely national operatic style, but in its place made Paris a centre of European opera, and the home of the somewhat cosmopolitan creation, French Grand Opera, in the nineteenth century. Thus French developments were brought into the main stream of opera to reform the Italian stage, as Wagner was later to bring German characteristics to reform the French.

In Jommelli we are dealing with a much more immediate influence on Gluck. Noverre, whose reform theories we have already examined, was ballet master to many of Jommelli's productions and the influence of the French ballet and chorus is apparent in their work. There is also much that is traditionally Italian in his operas, but a third important influence derives from the symphonic style of Vienna and Mannheim. When Jommelli returned to his native city of Naples after holding posts in Vienna and Stuttgart, his works failed, he was told, because of his 'foreign' style.

The arias are both the core of Jommelli's operas and the most conservative aspect of them. Jommelli still wrote 'singers' opera' and no opportunity is missed to introduce the splendid, brilliant, concerto-like movements which dominate the music of the drama. In form, these arias are generally less adventurous than those of Handel. The extended *da capo* form prevails, and the usual changes in the repeated first section are simply those that would make a more embellished run, a higher climax. Though they are often intensely dramatic within themselves, they hold up the action while contributing very little to characterization – which is, after all, the main justification for the introduction of arias into drama. They are usually based, musically and theatrically, on a static 'gesture' which the singer would hold during the entire length, a gesture which would not be impeded by the heavy eighteenth-century costumes and which would express the basic 'affection' of the whole movement. The initial musical phrase is more often than not of a formal, characterless nature:

EX. 3

and after the often very expressive middle section (expressive in a formalized idiom of chromatic sighs and scale-passage anger) the *da capo* is almost inevitable, the few occasions on which Jommelli omits it being sufficiently uninteresting in material to warrant their neglect. The arias are often preceded by a long ritornello for full orchestra, a Viennese symphony in effect, which helps to isolate the arias from the drama even more conclusively than the irrelevancies of the arias themselves.

The chorus is used as in Rameau for formal prayer scenes, as at the opening of *Fetonte*; in dramatic fragments; and combined in dance. The *secco* recitative is a great weakness, almost uniformly dull and very lengthy. It is in the accompanied recitative scenes that Jommelli makes his most significant developments. These are often intensely exciting. Jommelli uses them to carry the main climaxes of his operas, and these extended scenes, usually in dialogue and involving the chorus, differ completely from the formal *stromentato* preceding the main arias. The use of the orchestra, again, is symphonic. The wind instruments, particularly, are often used in the 'new manner': unmelodically, sustaining chords, producing an integrated sound. Solo passages, dialogue, and choruses are combined without regard to musical form, as if to make explicit the action portrayed in the continuous orchestral background. This procedure was scarcely improved upon by Gluck, and looks forward to Wagner for its ultimate development. One point which can have held no attraction for Gluck is that Jommelli's music becomes increasingly contrapuntal throughout his life. It is this complexity (almost always in the orchestral passages; Jommelli's idea of a vocal ensemble seems to consist

largely of duet style, and that no more than an aria with the coloratura in thirds and sixths) that made him unpopular in his own country,
the Neapolitans attributing it to his German sojourn. Certainly it seems
to stem from his awareness of the orchestra as a means to drama. But
Gluck's orchestral music is uniformly simpler, and uniformly more effective. Rameau lacked the simplicity of rhythm which makes Gluck's
slightest melodies striking; Jommelli lacked the simplicity both of texture
and of line, to the detriment of his attitude to aria and therefore to the
centre of opera itself.

Traetta was a younger man (1727–79), Jommelli being an exact contemporary of Gluck, and Rameau a whole generation older. Gluck's
late start and slow progress, however, accounted for the fact that
Traetta's most important operas were all contemporary with Gluck's
first reform works. Gluck must have known much of Traetta's work; he
conducted performances of his operas in Vienna, and his adopted
daughter's repertoire contained a number of pieces from them. Both
composers set *Iphigénies*, and both came under French influence – not of
the modern French stage of Noverre, but of the long-dead age of Lully
and Quinault. Traetta set Quinault's *Armide* in 1760. The libretto was
translated into Italian, partly by the ubiquitous Count Durazzo, as the
work was performed in Vienna. In the same year, at Parma, Traetta
composed a translation of Rameau's *Castor et Pollux* (*I Tindaridi*). All the
ballet *entrées* and chorus scenes were retained in the Italian versions, and
a strange mixture of conventions results.

Traetta generally abandons the Italian aria, and writes small-scale
airs called 'cavatas' or 'cavatinas', which approach the slight and form-
less airs in Rameau's opera, and also the more lyrical songs in Gluck's
Orfeo. Traetta has a stronger rhythmic sense than Rameau, or perhaps
merely a more modern rhythmic sense, and seems to favour the $\frac{6}{8}$
rhythms of Neapolitan and Sicilian music. His most attractive gift is
sheer melodic grace, in which he approaches Mozart and leaves Gluck
far behind; but as Gluck has frequently shown, both in words and music,
in opera such a gift can be a fault, or at least a hindrance. Traetta's
drama often loses power by the continuous lyricism of much of his style:
for example, Orestes' plea for pity in *Iphigenia* is accompanied by a
cantabile 'cello solo! Traetta's musical style is far more Italian than
Gluck's, although he worked so often within the framework of French
opera.

The chief weaknesses in Traetta's work are due to his conservative librettists who are responsible for the time-wasting convention of the confidants. We notice the superfluity of these essentially neo-classical roles chiefly in comparison with Gluck's operas which eventually overthrow them: the whole *rapport* between Iphigenia and her priestesses is considerably weakened when their sympathizing function is usurped by Dori, the confidante assigned by Coltellini to provoke Iphigenia to conversation. There are several missed opportunities for dramatic conciseness, above all in the furies' choruses in Traetta's *Iphigenia*, which contain some tremendously forceful rhythms and cumulative climaxes, but which lack the force of brevity of Gluck's choruses: the furies sing too long, and the listener is led to examine the music they sing – well worth examination – rather than to remain struck by the initial effect of it. Thus they lose their terror. Perhaps if Traetta had happened to collaborate with Calzabigi, or at least with a librettist with sympathies for the reform, he would have made a more significant contribution to eighteenth-century opera. As it is, he provides an excellent answer to those who regret Gluck's lack of melodic gift. This gift took Traetta no farther than his librettists: Gluck's librettists took him farther without it.

Chapter four

Gluck's Development of the Aria

OPERA in Gluck's lifetime underwent the second significant transformation since its invention. The first phase, covering the development from Monteverdi to Handel, resulted in the widely travelled *opera seria* which by Handel's time had become the most important musical form in Europe. This musical style spread faster than any style had travelled before, and yet the result was never international: 'late Baroque' opera remained strongly Italian with both the richness and limitations we expect to find in nationalist music, and consequently stifled or hindered the development of an indigenous school in those countries where it was most fully accepted. This first period of opera saw one overwhelming development – the aria. Within a century, the whole nature of opera as the Camerata had conceived it changed from an amateurish and impractical piece of idealism into a natural musical form. The late Baroque aria itself, tantamount to almost the whole achievement of early eighteenth-century opera, is a magnificently fundamental and satisfying structure, which we will examine in this chapter; because of these very qualities it was bound to be discarded, since it could not be developed.

Gluck's work opens the second phase of opera, but here it is impossible to move from one single great name to another; thus we must designate this period as reaching from Gluck, Traetta, and, in retrospect, Rameau, to ultimately both Wagner and Debussy. But opera is so varied by genre and nationality in the late eighteenth and the nineteenth centuries that there is no single and complete evolution to compare with the pattern of the seventeenth century. Gluck's work plays an important part in the development. Whether it is witness to, or cause of the reform (which convenient expression will now be seen to imply no more than the beginnings of the second phase, albeit turbulent beginnings) we have already shown to be controversial and, in all honesty, unanswerable. We can, however, trace in his operas more clearly and continuously than in the work of any other single composer, both the acquisition of the late Baroque Italian style and eventually the rejection of this and the creation of a new operatic convention. In this reform, and therefore in Gluck's works, the fate of the aria is of paramount importance.

It is now necessary to describe the aria form which played such an important part in the reform controversies. The high point of development which it reached at this period must surely stand as perfect for all time: it would be impossible to go farther within the limits of this convention without destroying the nature of the form. The whole point lies, as with all music of this age, in the balance between expression and form.

The ternary structure was by no means new, but the *da capo* aria was one of the earliest examples of it in which the repeat element became formally inevitable, rather than a brief reprise of the opening in order to give the appearance of a 'circular' work. The greatest talent of the early eighteenth-century composer lay in selecting not only a situation but also words and musical themes in which two contrasting ideas could be convincingly expressed side by side, with the first idea not only predominating, but returning to conclude the matter. In fact, the composer had control of only one of these requirements. The limited scope for dramatically justifiable use of this exacting form will be seen to be vastly disproportionate to the number of arias produced. Driven by these conventions of aria form, heroes contradicted themselves and suffered the vagaries of heroines who had to change their minds twice at least in the course of a short aria – hence the large number of middle sections beginning with 'but'. On the whole, the faults lay with the librettists, and the composers adapted the music as well as possible to the situation. Also the increasing flexibility of style in vocal music received considerable stimulus from the popularity of this form, of which, it is important to add, there exist many perfect and wholly appropriate examples from the most insignificant composers of the time. First consistently used by Scarlatti from a little before the turn of the century, and sounding distinctly archaic in Jommelli's mid-century operas, the aria both in opera and cantata influenced practically all the composers writing within the period. It made a positive contribution to music after that date, too, for the intimate expression of Gluck's, and later accompanied recitative, derives in no small part from the more freely composed middle sections of the *da capo* aria.

The most masterly composer of this form in the period was undoubtedly Handel. But as the subtleties he incorporated to adapt the old 'type' arias to his own flexible and perceptive characterization increased, his adherence to the form decreased: scarcely half the arias in his late oratorios can be described without qualification as *da capo*. The changes he introduced show him as one of the most forward-looking composers of his age. But nowhere do his developments foreshadow Gluck's. The dichotomy between them is apparent in every consideration – character, inclination, direction, and quality of talent. How Gluck could seek to recommend himself to the composer of *Giulio Cesare* and *Theodora*, with the characterless material and transparent construction of *Artamene* and *La Caduta dei Giganti*, it is hard to see! But Gluck doubtless came under Handel's influence at an early stage, and must have realized the unbridgeable gulf between them, for he never aspired to imitate Handel's last and most dramatic works, although he paid tribute to the older man throughout his life, saying of a portrait of Handel which hung for many years in his bedroom: 'There is the portrait of the most inspired master of our art; when I open my eyes in the morning I look upon him with reverential awe, and acknowledge him as such.'

Gluck's earliest operas, however, contain little trace of an awareness of Handel's qualities. Under his apprenticeship to Sammartini he produced with varying degrees of collaboration and plagiarism his first ten operas. Of these, little more than half the arias remain. Their publication in isolated numbers or small collections based on the repertory of a famous singer stresses the public's attitude to Italian opera: if the essence of the work was not in the arias then it was nowhere at all. All that has come down to us from these incomplete scores is very run-of-the-mill work. The ritornelli provide a simple (three-part, two-part, or even unison) presentation of the main tune, which tune sounds in these early operas at times stiff and awkward, at others obvious and ready-made. Gluck was out to comply, not reform, and his most successful arias at this stage are those which achieve a wholly Italian fluency, like this regular *da capo* aria which opens Gluck's third opera, *Demofoonte* (Milan 1742):

Demófoonte
2 Horns & Strings

It is a successful aria, in an unambitious way, and it succeeds by virtue
of its rhythm and melodic inevitability. The ritornello is effective because it sounds slick and appropriate played by strings – and here we
come across one of the most important influences on Gluck's early style,
the Italian symphony.

Sammartini was as forward-looking, as 'modern' a composer in the
instrumental field as Handel was in opera. And for instrumental music
to shake off the *concerto grosso* style meant that the new symphony was
indeed modern. The concerto style had suggested the beginnings of
seventeenth-century instrumental music, and through its development
orchestral music had found its feet for the first time. The symphony
inherited the natural violin idiom and basic dance metres of the concerto, but lightened the language with the brief, bubbling, patter-aria
style of the recently developed *opera buffa*. This was the Italian symphony
– and the style remained the essence of all symphonic finales before
Beethoven – complementary with the German development of the symphony in Mannheim, which lacked both the lightness and the melodic
style while working out a far more varied instrumentation and new
forms.

Sammartini was one of the first composers of the symphony. It may
be thought that the very violence with which Haydn denied his influence
indicates some kind of relationship between them as symphonic composers. The relationship between Gluck's orchestral music and Sammartini's is obvious, however, although the subject of no recorded
opinion. All that is clear-cut and vigorous in Gluck's early music seems
to spring from the similar style of his teacher and also, incidentally, from
Pergolesi. Comparisons with this Neapolitan composer can be made
frequently from Gluck's Milan operas and later from his *opéras-comiques*.
The common ground between them is chiefly that of rhythm – the
detached, pithy rhythmic phrase seen in this aria, again from *Demofoonte*, which opens without a ritornello:

EX. 5

Demofoonte

T'in-ten-do, t'in-ten - do in –gra - ta, in - gra - ta

and which also harps on two semitones of the minor scale (between the
fifth and sixth degrees and leading note to tonic) giving the Neapolitan

colouring which is usual in Pergolesi. The middle section of this (*da capo*)
aria is in much the same style; at –

EX. 6

we can see both the insistence on semitones and the very brief, self-
contained phrases that Gluck assembles to construct his vocal line.

The instrumental style, then, is the basis of the aria at this early point.
Numerous ritornelli open with an idiomatic phrase or with a curt motif
used in a truly orchestral manner, like the nervously energetic opening
of 'Care pupille' which Gluck transferred from one of the Milan operas
to *La Caduta* in 1746. The voice enters with a modified outline of the
instrumental figure. It is a powerful aria, one of the most outstanding
from Gluck's early period. The key range is greater than in the majority
of arias from these works, and in the middle section there is a most
expressive little climax, obvious enough viewed simply from the harmonic point of view, and achieved easily within the bounds of logical
tune construction, yet it is one of the smoothest and most finished
passages from the period. (EX. 7)

This aria is also one of the first instances of Gluck's undoubted awareness of his own good points. For in the incredibly large number of self-
borrowings throughout his life, which range from a couple of bars of a
ballet movement inserted in a passage of recitative to some of his largest
and most memorable arias taken unrevised from one work to another,
Gluck's talent for choosing only his finest passages to perpetuate makes
one wonder at the uncritical turn of mind that could allow weaker
passages to exist at all in finished versions.

In the operas he wrote at Milan, Gluck was most successful when most
conventional. We can unfortunately have no very reliable idea of the
quality of the musical drama of these first ten operas, as only *Ipermestra*
(1744) has come down to us complete. From this work, however, it
seems that we have lost little in the suppression of the recitative in the
remaining operas: there is no indication that the drama is ever worked
out in time or key scales larger than that of the aria itself. To what
extent this was caused by audience apathy to recitative, and management economy on choruses, it is fascinating to speculate. This piece-by-
piece construction of the opera is probably one of the most important

EX. 7

differences between Italian opera such as Gluck was writing at this time
and the contemporary French opera; Rameau already had acquired a
sense of musical architecture in constructing continuous scenes with

binding ritornelli, chorus refrains, and dances, and with consciously chosen key relationships. Whether this be cause or effect, Rameau's units are shorter, the aria is nothing but a momentary point of lyrical repose in what is essentially *l'action*; the time-scale of each scene is often no longer than that of a single aria by Gluck, and the structure is there-fore easily grasped by the audience. All Baroque music, all music before the Viennese form-building symphonists, tended to use these miniature periods, and Gluck's extended structures in his last operas are far closer to Rameau's methods than to the symphonically derived forms of Mozart's ensemble scenes.

The recurrence of aria material from these early works in a com-position as mature as, for example, *Telemacco* (1765) gives us the clue to the fate of the Italian aria in later opera. Material from *Sofonisba* (1744) and *Ippolito* (1745) recurs in both acts of *Telemacco*. The numbers in question are Telemachus' 'Se per entro alla nera foresta', which, after its opening tag of rising fourths, moves into the powerful arpeggio phrase which reappears consistently throughout a lifetime's composition of spirit evocations:

EX. 8

Se per en-tro al-la ne-ra for-es -ta   Om - bra mesta del pad-re t'a-gi-ri

Circe's accompanied recitative before the aria 'Dall' orrido soggiorno' shows another device which had appeared frequently in the early operas – the syncopated, expansive presentation of harmonic progressions; a similar introduction also appears in Ulysses' aria 'Freme gonfio di tor-bide spume'. The voice enters with a bold, fanfare-like tune which is rewritten from 'Ah già parmi' in Act III of *Ippolito*. All of these musical ideas can be found in *Alceste* in the great aria 'Ombre, Larve' towards the end of the first act. Herein lies the admirable achievement of Gluck's developing use of the aria: in the Milan operas this broad and weighty style was completely conventional; it might appear in three or four arias in the course of one opera, to moderate but not overwhelming effect, since its context was a chain of arias of equal length and possibly equal brilliance. By *Telemacco*, the arias are still the main vehicle for musical ex-pression, but this particular style had become attached, if not to the supernatural, at least to the most important moments in human expression.

(*Telemacco* is in many ways Gluck's most highly coloured opera; a new expansive style is seen in the gradual building up of the climax to Circe's 'Dall' orrido soggiorno', and some of Gluck's rare coloratura – rare in serious operas, as opposed to festival works – is given to Circe, his most exotic and fully drawn heroine. Empty vocal virtuosity is seldom found in Gluck's most significant operas, perhaps because, like Haydn and unlike Mozart, his own character had little in common with performer composers who alone are able to hold virtuosity in respect, and compel that respect from their audience.) But in *Alceste*, with only two arias in the whole of the first act which are formally detached from the continuous musical texture, this aria stands out as a most powerful and striking expression of Alcestis' character, the more so since this ceremonial style is balanced against the near-recitative intimacy of the 'middle section'.

This, then, is what becomes of the Italian aria. Gluck wrote examples of it throughout his life, freeing it from a too mechanical and sectional construction though preserving the counterbalance of two emotions – and therefore of two styles – which is as much an integral part of it as is some sort of *da capo* feeling, however freely this is carried out. Gluck also involved the orchestra increasingly in the texture and style of the aria. The orchestra was all but ignored in Italy except as an appropriate accompaniment or introduction, but in French and German opera it expanded and was increasingly exploited as it grew. But instead of being the main vehicle for the musical unfolding of the plot, the aria was eventually used by Gluck only where it was credible that a character might step outside the chorus-recitative-*arioso* tissue to involve the complications of form and the 'artificial' manner. In short, the arias in the reform operas most often occur where heightened poetry or song would be acceptable in a spoken play, for lyrical reflection, serenade, soliloquy, and spells and invocation of the underworld. This usage of the large-scale aria (which the Italian aria always remains) can be seen in *Alceste* and in both *Iphigénies*. A typical example is the prayer aria which opens the last act of *Iphigénie en Tauride* (1779), 'Je t'implore et je tremble', which occurred previously in both *Telemacco* and in *Antigono* (1756). Becoming increasingly impressive as the proximity of other arias decreases, this 'grand aria' seems more grand in its reform context.

In *Orfeo* and *Paride* we have frequent examples of the 'song' context in opera. The use of song in spoken drama is a fascinating subject, and no less so is this special motivation of aria in sung drama. It is apparently the most natural way to give a character the chance to sing. And yet it presents a set of problems of realism that are not aroused by even the lengthiest *da capo* interpolation into swiftly moving action.

The chief problem arises because to introduce song into continuously sung opera is to risk losing the audience's acceptance of the whole convention of drama in music. If that, the listener might well reason, is a song which has been composed and learned and is performed to an audience on the stage, how does it differ from this aria which the same character sings a few minutes later, now meant to be a spontaneous expression, perhaps even an aside, sung in the presence of the same characters? To give an example outside Gluck, in *Figaro* the audience must be able to distinguish between 'Voi che sapete', the song, and 'Non so più', the aria. And it is not only other arias, but also the surrounding music – recitative and chorus – that is problematic. The composer has two realities to convey; the song must sound a convincing song, while aria and recitative are to be accepted as normal speech. This is usually solved by making the music of the song noticeably lighter than the style of the rest of the work. Mozart, for example, gives a guitar-like texture to accompany Don Giovanni's serenade as he also does to 'Voi che sapete'; and Gluck uses a similarly unobtrusive accompaniment to Paris's song 'Quegli occhi belli' around which most of the third act of *Paride ed Elena* is constructed. He uses the same device to accompany Orpheus' pleas to the furies in Act II of *Orfeo*. Characterization provides another difficulty with the song aria: whether to align the style of the song with the remainder of the music for that character or to emphasize its self-sufficiency by a marked contrast. It is not often that the result seems worth risking the relative realism of the whole opera.

Gluck, however, wrote two operas based entirely on the introduction of song into opera. *Orfeo* and *Paride ed Elena* might well have been called *drames lyriques*, with *Echo et Narcisse*, for they fulfil the title far more completely than does the latter work. The similarities between these two 'lyrical dramas' have not previously been adequately set out. The essential difference between these operas and *Alceste* and the *Iphigénies* lies in the nature of their plots: both the latter heroines are chiefly involved with religion and state, at least to the extent that we see them acting ceremonially, facing Corneille-like clashes of inclination and duty in spite of their very human portrayal as women. ('Vous n'avez plus de Roi, je n'ai plus de parents' – the personal situation in its context of political implications.) By comparison, the tragedy of Orpheus and the intrigues of Paris are wholly personal situations. The musical style must show this difference, and in fact *Paride* is the first opera in which Gluck claimed to have created a scheme of characterization on which such intimate psychological drama must depend. Gluck himself is well aware of the contrast between *Alceste* and *Paride*, making in the dedication of the score of the latter the following comment: 'This is no matter of a wife who is to lose her husband, and who, to save him, courageously invokes the infernal gods in a dread forest in the very depths of night; who concerns herself with the future of her sons even on her own death-bed, where she has to take leave of the husband she adores. Here we have the case of a young lover who is shown in contrast to a wayward but lovely woman. . . . I strove to find a variety of colour in this music, illustrating the different characters of the two nations of Phrygia and Sparta by contrasting the rough and savage nature of the latter with the wholly delicate and yielding character of the former.'

Orfeo lacks this dominating contrast of race and therefore of two musical styles. Perhaps it gains by doing so, for in seeking to illuminate the differences in *Paride*, Gluck seems often to produce less attractive work from a purely musical point of view; though he defends himself against just this criticism with his credo that the greatest beauties of melody and harmony become defects and imperfections when out of place. The opening chorus of *Paride*, 'Non sdegnare, O bella Venere', is not trivial, as it has sometimes been adjudged – certainly no more so than the hymns to Diana in *Iphigénie en Tauride* and considerably more substantial than the majority of final choruses in Italian opera of this period. It is, however, something in the nature of a shock. Neither Orpheus nor Paris is a conventional hero. Orpheus is rightly cast as a castrato for an age in which that voice implied the deification of vocal art: Orpheus' character is simply that. Thus, that the drama of *Orfeo* should be a lyrical drama unfolding in song, not aria, is in itself a dramatic stroke.

Paris is less simple. The libretto removes the adulterous nature of the episode. But history appears to have decreed that passion for a dead woman is more respectable than for a living one. And Paris is affected, sophisticated, and, anachronistically, a courtly lover; these characteristics are faithfully portrayed in the soft Phrygian music of both the choruses of his followers and his own songs. As with Orpheus, lyricism is a quality of his character, and so Paris sings: songs.

They resemble the *Orfeo* first-act songs in that they have no ritornelli

and proceed almost syllabically. The first five-bar period of Paris' song
'O del mio dolce ardor' pictures the broken-up 'sighing' phrases,
intimate ornaments, and Neapolitan semitone phrasing:

EX. 9

His second air adds to this the appogiatura softening of the melodic line –

EX. 10

Both pieces begin with a bar of unassuming and unmelodic accompaniment, similar to Orpheus' lute accompaniments in Act II of *Orfeo*. Paris
continues in this style throughout the opera. Helen, on the other hand,
sings two fine arias in the grand manner (but only two such arias for a
heroine in 1770!) full of the athletic vigour of her country's characterization according to Gluck, and seen most effectively in the ballet scenes
in the second act.

In both *Orfeo* and *Paride*, and indeed in all the operas of this late
period, the result of thinning out the arias is apparent in the increased
use of recitative. Such an upheaval of Italian aria-opera could only be
achieved when the recitative was of sufficient musical content to sustain
a large part of the action. The grand aria is retained for use once or
twice in an opera, and in a few appropriate circumstances song takes its
place. What is left to the composer for the many situations which in the
course of the plot require musical comment and that unfolding of
emotion for which there is no space in the flow of recitative?

For this purpose Gluck established the small aria, derived from both
the small-scale arias of Traetta and the simple numbers of *opéra-comique*.
These are often similar to the songs in *Orfeo* and *Paride*, though they can
employ a fuller ritornello and conventional ternary form; but the chief
difference is that they occur in a genuinely aria context, that is, arising
out of the character's need to reveal himself, rather than from the more
'external' motivation – a goddess to be hymned, furies to be appeased –
which gives rise to the songs. These small arias are very important to the

swift unfolding of the drama in Gluck's best works. They stand among his most personal creations together with the lyrical *arioso* fragments which sometimes approach them very closely in function, both devices being wholly symptomatic of the continuity of reform opera.

But in considering *Orfeo* and *Paride* and the song in opera, we have broken the chronological thread of this chapter. To find Gluck's earliest use of the form we have called the small aria we must look to the most interesting and formative period of his life: between 1755 and 1767; in other words, from the beginning of Gluck's collaboration with Durazzo to the opening of his last period of almost uninterrupted reform master-pieces, with *Alceste*. This period is most easily identified as that of the *opéras-comiques*, though these had been imported into Vienna from about 1752. Gluck's earliest known contribution is *L'Isle de Merlin* in 1758, but it is very possible that to most of the works he is known to have conducted (beginning with *Les Amours Champêtres* in 1755) Gluck added airs, en-riched those he orchestrated, and in other ways thoroughly assimilated their simple style.

Before these works, however, came the first-fruit of Durazzo's artistic friendship, *L'Innocenza Giustificata*. This contains three fine arias from the early Italian operas but for our purpose two smaller movements are far more interesting – probably Gluck's first use of this intimate style. The first is Flaminia's aria 'A'giorni suoi la sorte', a gentle duet with flutes, within the small time-scale of many of Traetta's arias. The second small aria is sung by Claudia as she is about to be sacrificed. (EX. 11)

And Gluck does not neglect to repeat this dramatic touch for Orestes also on the point of death. This utter melodic simplicity in a major key (often G major) is also frequently found in the later operas to express grief.

These two arias are hardly significant in *L'Innocenza*, an unequal work which is still dominated by the grand-scale and brilliant-style Italian arias, seen in the two self-plagiarisms from *Issipile* and *Artamene*. But in the *opéras-comiques* this scale of writing is the normal language of the drama. There is, of course, rarely opportunity for such subtlety and intimacy of expression in the *opéras-comiques*. The spurious operas, before *L'Isle de Merlin*, which have sometimes been attributed to Gluck, are characterized by an uninhibited vigour, frequent clumsiness of phrase lengths and tonality, and general disregard for the correct accentuation of the text, the latter almost certainly arising from the frequent use of dance tunes, or at least a pre-composed melody, beneath which the text

EX. II

had to be fitted. At their worst they had a harsh originality which must have sounded refreshing to the Schönbrunn audience, cushioned for so long on Metastasian elegance:

EX. 12

At best, they had a direct expression and consequently lucid characterization which could not but be communicated to any composer undertaking their presentation.

EX. 13

Opéra-comique had started, like Italian *opera buffa*, as a parody of serious opera. But it had never reached such a high musical standard as the Italian form, and at the time it reached Vienna had stagnated in two dramatic conventions: either the plot was based on Oriental fantasy, which showed associations with both Italian opera (Gluck's own *Le Cinesi*) and the later German *Singspiel* (*Die Entführung*), or else it dealt with more or less contemporary life but with stylized characters from the *commedia del arte* tradition made familiar to us through Molière. It is from this second genre that we can trace a significant nineteenth-century development: *opéra-comique*, *opera buffa*, and *Singspiel* all presented the audience with scenes of servant life, originally in parody of, and eventually combining with, the exalted characters inherent in the Greek tradition of serious opera. (If in England the reaction from serious opera caused the compilers of *The Beggars' Opera* to set the plot among people not of servant class but of realistic 'low life', it is because the *commedia del arte* had never become indigenous; but the same trend of parodying contrast can be seen.) We can follow the development of the *buffa* characters simply in the increased importance, resourcefulness, and character of Figaro, compared with the earlier type portrayed in Leporello. But after the French Revolution Figaro pales beside Massaniello, the hero of the people becomes a feature of French grand opera, and the dichotomy between the *seria* type of aria and the simple air from comic opera is preserved in the duality of styles which distinguishes the social status of the dramatis personae of most nineteenth-century operas.

Even if we regard 'A'giorni suoi la sorte' and 'Ah rivolgi' as the first steps in the search for simplicity – and it is a real temptation in assessing the style of a revolutionary artist to read a completely exaggerated significance into such deviations – it was obviously in the *opéras-comiques* that Gluck first met and used the simple vitality he was later to introduce into *opera seria*. His earliest efforts are the most elementary. The first number in *L'Isle de Merlin* is completely within the bounds of the 'folk' idiom of the original operas with their authentic anonymous French airs:

EX. 14

and this number immediately follows an *ouverture descriptive* on which Gluck based the prelude to *Iphigénie en Tauride*! It is the prevalence of this folk style well on into the composed *opéras-comiques* that gives us the best insight into the nature of the company of actors engaged to perform these works. Only gradually are the subtleties of chromaticism and graces introduced; and, more important from the point of view of the composer, only gradually do the airs become an integral part of the plot. In *L'Arbre Enchanté* (1759) the airs are still for the most part used merely as interludes, complementary to the dialogue which runs quite continuously without them. This opera introduces some new devices, however, which show a more individual handling of the arias than in *L'Isle de Merlin* or *La Fausse Esclave*: the canonic entry of the voice with the violins in the air 'Près de l'objet qui m'enflamme', for example. The aria 'Du jeune objet que j'adore' contains a small instance of the language of serious opera, in the 'aspirated' treatment of the sighs in the line 'Entens mes soupirs, puissant Dieu des plaisirs'. And in Thomas's aria 'Je prétens que dans ce jour tout ici se rejouisse', Gluck is developing his own *buffa* style, akin to the Italian in its constant quaver movement, but with a character of its own, consistent with the 'French' style of the remainder of the work. True to his character, Gluck was consciously blending national traditions to evolve his personal idiom.

This *buffa* treatment of a bass role also appears in *L'Ivrogne Corrigé* (1760), one of the most fully composed of the unrevised comic operas. It has been by far the most frequently revived of these works, probably because of the fine vigorous quality of the melodies, full of personality and clear-cut characterization, and also because of the subject, which is more likely to appeal to a modern sense of humour than either the *commedia del arte* vein of eloping wards and foolish old guardians or the Oriental extravaganzas.

Although the most dramatic moments arise in the ensemble movements which are irrelevant to this chapter, a number of the airs are worth mentioning: the 'preview' of 'Che faro' in Cléon's 'Avec nous il prit naissance', or Mathurine's splendid drunken song 'Ah que j'ai bu du bon vin!' This number and most of the second act show Gluck making music a more essential component of the drama: characters no longer repeat in verse and song what they have just spoken in prose. The inevitability of genuine folk song is still to be found in two of the gayest airs in the opera, Pluton's 'Vous n'aurez que la bastonnade' and Lucas's air in the finale: 'Allons, morbleu! Point de chagrin.' From among these – and even from among the very nearly wholly serious fury scenes – Mathurine's aria 'O puissant Dieu' stands out as an intensely serious number, worthy to take its place in any of the reform operas. Gluck's

success with these *opéras-comiques* arose in no small part from his ability
to write with compelling realism even for the trivial episodes and insignificant characters in these scenes of contemporary life.

The later *opéras-comiques* employ a much more intricate style. *Le Cadi
Dupé*, for example, written only a year before *Orfeo*, contains chromaticism which requires a far higher standard of technique in its performance than that of the earlier works. The actors must by now have
become singers. This passage –

EX. 15

occurs at the beginning of an *air dialogué* designed to contrast the
characters of Zelmire, flirtatious and feminine, and the Cadi, ponderous
and unsubtle. Gluck does not, however, adopt this 'composed' rather
than 'folk' style consistently in these works until the last of the group,
La Rencontre Imprévue, in 1764. His blend of the simplicity of a French air
in a thoroughly manufactured tune can be illustrated in the first number
of this long, and indeed diffuse opera:

EX. 16

Most of the numbers in this opera are small *da capo* arias rather than
French airs; some are not small, and introduce coloratura passages
(Rezia's 'Ah! qu'il est doux de se revoir') in the Italian manner so
familiar to Gluck. The composer and his audiences had mutually rejected their surfeit of simplicity.

The *opéras-comiques* are attractive works, many of them as well worth
revival today as they were popular in their own time. But their relevance
to the present topic lies not in their intrinsic interest so much as in their
contribution to the last, most mature operas that immediately followed

the period of their composition. What, then, is the extent of their contribution? Certainly the small air replaces all but a few of the arias in the Paris operas, and is featured as a special technique in *Orfeo* and *Paride*. But the airs in *Iphigénie en Aulide* are a very different matter from the simple structures in *L'Ivrogne Corrigé* although it is from these that the former took their shape. The folk-like airs of the comic operas were unsuitable in more serious contexts because of the very directness of their melodic line. This was incapable of expressing the subtleties of the emotions of tragedy, being primarily instrumental in character, and often, as we have mentioned, a dance tune with words composed to fit the metre. Thus the short arias in the reform operas, while having the apparent simplicity and proportions of those from the *opéras-comiques*, are in reality a different genre.

The small aria does not appear immediately with the reform. We have shown it to be a special case in *Orfeo*, arising out of the nature of the subject and the character of the hero. It is not featured in *Alceste*, a chorus opera *par excellence*, and in *Paride ed Elena* the usage is again prompted by the externals of the plot. It is not until *Iphigénie en Aulide* that Gluck first achieves a quickly moving yet continuously lyrical drama through the medium of this informal movement. And here we have the possible incentive of a desire to mould his style on the traditional French opera, which Burney, at least, thinks to be a paramount formative influence on the Paris operas. Certainly Gluck's catalogue of works shows a desire to please the differing audiences for which his operas were destined – the so-called lapses of *Il Trionfo di Clelia*, the *Prologo*, and *Le Feste d'Apollo* (all post *Orfeo*) being no more nor less commendable because they were attempts to please the public of Bologna, Florence, and Parma respectively; even the latter, sometime working-ground of Traetta, being considerably more conservative than the capitals of Vienna and Paris. The influence of the opera of Lully and Rameau had indeed had its effect on Gluck: but this was earlier, in 1762, and Calzabigi was the channel through which it reached him. Hence the new concern with visual effect in *Orfeo* and subsequent works, the tableau architecture of the scenes, the ballets, and above all the chorus. But these were soon made subservient to Gluck's own dramatic ideas, for in the long rehearsals for *Iphigénie en Aulide* Gluck had to teach the Paris chorus to act.

Iphigénie en Aulide, then, is a product of the concurrence of Gluck's own development with congenial artistic traditions. The fact that it contained much that was new for Paris is borne out by the famous six months of rehearsal necessary to produce it for the French stage. And yet, apart from *Echo et Narcisse*, a sprawling profusion of airs and dances, it is the most truly French of all Gluck's operas, and by far the most indebted to Rameau. It contains some of the closest blending of recitative with aria that Gluck ever wrote: it is impossible, for example, to class Agamemnon's magnificent opening prayer (borrowed from *Telemacco*) decisively as either recitative or aria fragment. Three bars of ritornello introduce the perfect example of the small aria, 'Brillant auteur de la lumière'. Fidelity to the natural rhythms of the text gives it the same flexibility and sensitivity we find in Rameau, especially at the cadences:

EX. 17

This may be compared with the only similar small aria in *Iphigénie en Tauride*. (EX. 18)

It is in music like this that Gluck most nearly approaches the spirit of the Camerata, in the exact imitation of spoken declamation and with a freedom of metre that contrasts strongly with the dance airs of *opéra-comique*.

The detail Gluck lavishes on these miniatures is the more surprising in the face of his declared aims which scorned mere musical detail in the interest of broad dramatic effect. The aria 'Peuvent-ils ordonner qu'un père de sa main' (*Iphigénie en Aulide*) is a well-known example of Gluck's

EX. 18

Iphigénie en Tauride

D'une i - mage, hé las, trop ché-ri . . e, j'aime en-core à m'en - tre - te - nir; mon

â - me se plait à nour - rir

subtle use of the orchestra – the oboe 'cri plaintif de la nature', which is anticipated in the Neapolitan semitones of the vocal line, and which illustrates not only the one sympathetic aspect of Agamemnon's character here but also the whole tenderness and sensitivity of most of the music in this opera.

These small arias do not end: their cadential phrase is developed or repeated to lead into the next number, often an accompanied recitative. In the aria of Agamemnon mentioned in the last paragraph, the final phrase of the voice part, 'Je n'obéirai point à cet ordre inhumain', is taken up by the orchestra and repeated to form a very brief pause before the ensuing recitative for Calchas. In this way Gluck builds up long scenes of continuous music, and continuous dramatic tension. Even when the continuity is not required by the speed of the action, Gluck is obviously thinking in much larger formal units than before. Scene 5 of the first act of *Iphigénie* introduces Clytemnestra and Iphigenia amid a chain of dances, with short dance airs in the Lullian manner (*air gai*, *air gracieux*), a strange and ironic introduction to one of the greatest classical heroines in opera. The succession of variable tempi and metres is also found occasionally. Iphigenia's soliloquy 'Hélas mon coeur sensible et tendre' is an example of this, very near to the borderline between recitative and aria.

There is nothing so close to Rameau in *Iphigénie en Tauride*. Apart from 'D'une image, hélas', already quoted, the music reverts to the formality of a more Italian style: the rhythms are instrumental rather than dictated by the poem, and there are few ambiguities of style between aria and recitative. In the first *Iphigénie* we can see the small aria giving way to an increasing use of recitative towards the end of the opera. The very lyricism of the style of the arias precludes their use to convey great dramatic situations. Probably their most appropriate use is at the beginning of an opera where the characterization – potential drama – is usually more important than dramatic events, which take over at the climax. And certainly few musical styles can reveal character quite so completely as this.

As a medium for lucid exposition of character and a contribution towards faster-moving action, the small aria was among Gluck's greatest achievements; many influences worked towards its evolution, but the result was a very personal idiom, superbly suited to Gluck's dramatic methods – perhaps uniquely so, for it seems to have died with him.

It is important to remember that Gluck's development of the aria is by no means equivalent to a growth of style from the Italian to the French. There are no forms used by him during his earliest period of composition that do not reappear to the very end of his life; and he nowhere recants his earliest compositions, although they are of the same dramatic method he condemns in the prefaces. The constant self-plagiarisms which persist even in *Echo et Narcisse* are incompatible with a rapidly or at least decisively developing personal style. And yet the early operas are very different from the reform group. The function of the aria has changed in the latter operas, and the new forms were created to convey this change of emphasis. Gluck's powers of characterization make immense strides during his *opéra-comique* period. It is also during this series that he seems to realize in its simplest form the relationship between arias and the plot: we see them gradually becoming more indispensable to the spoken dialogue, and less interchangeable between operas; while we could easily exchange arias between the pairs of lovers in *L'Ivrogne* and *L'Arbre Enchanté*, with little loss, characters like Mathurine, Zelmire, Vertigo, however insignificant plot-wise, command a musical personality of more individuality than the majority of Gluck's characters from the early Italian operas.

In the reform operas the new function of the aria and the new richness of characterization go hand in hand, for they are both caused by the same new factor: the tremendous expansion of recitative in style, flexibility, and usage gave the aria a freedom it had lacked since Scarlatti, it being no longer required to undertake the entire musical portrayal of the drama. The result lies in the greater realism and dramatic sense of the reform operas. Gluck's development of the aria consisted not only of the variety he gave to the form itself, but also to the context. Dr Burney wrote: 'Gluck's music is so truly dramatic that the airs and scenes, which have the greatest effect on the stage, are cold or rude in a concert. The situation, context, and interest, gradually excited in the audience, give them their force and energy.' Gluck's development of the aria could only come about through its dethronement from the pinnacle it commanded in early eighteenth-century opera: by recitative.

Chapter five

Gluck's Development of Recitative

RECITATIVE is the most fugitive aspect of opera, changing in style and function with almost every composer, and reflecting the entire history of opera in the course of its various mutations. It embraced originally the whole concept of opera. Since all reformers of opera have cried 'Back to the Greeks!' (or 'Back to the Camerata!') it is particularly important to understand the creation of opera from the already existing recitative style, in monody – a style which was no more than an oversophisticated vocal idiom symptomatic of the end of an era, a *reductio ad absurdum* of a search for expression and clarity of word-setting, while at the same time ushering in the *nuove musiche*.

At the point at which the Camerata took it up, monody was regarded as a form of heightened speech, its characteristics being a harmonically conceived tune, profusely ornamented, the ornaments rendering it virtually unmetrical, and underlining the affective interpretation of the text. Hitherto, most vocal music had played the part of an intensified form of speech. Together with dance music, and unlike the new concerto-symphonic forms of the succeeding centuries, it was almost always functional music, in the liturgy or on stage, replacing the spoken word but not adding to it.

Recitative carries on this purpose in opera. Originally conceived as a highly emotional medium, its role was soon robbed of its expressive highlights by the more lyrical *arioso* style, and was then further reduced as the aria grew into its position of dominance. That recitative formed the whole essence of the first operas serves to show how strictly relevant these works were. A hundred and fifty years later recitative had indeed gone down in the world of opera. But opera had become undeniably a more natural musical form.

Recitative is probably the least natural musical entity in opera. It deliberately avoids the lyrical and the rhythmic – two, surely, of the most spontaneous features of any style – and commits itself to achieve a most unmusical end, that of imitating speech. But because recitative in some shape is indispensable to opera, its style must be reconciled to the normal language of music used in the remainder of the operatic forms. It is indispensable while opera has any plot at all to have some kind of music in which to convey the mere mechanics of the action. To give an extreme example, Puccini could not make Pinkerton offer Sharpless a 'Milch Punch o Whiskey' in the same musical language that is subsequently used to depict the betrayed Butterfly. For another reason, something different from the aria style is needed – something briefer, barer, and with no possibility of a word being lost – to set a tense dialogue such as the one where Iphigenia learns of the fate of her family (*Tauride*, Act II, scene 5).

The need for such a style, functional but still consistent with the main stream of expressive music, is one of the toughest problems in opera, and each composer has faced it in a different way. The development of recitative is the history of the search for the best solution. When composers failed to acknowledge the problem, or required of opera something less than a continuous musical form, the result was the *secco* recitative of mid-eighteenth-century opera which could be replaced by the spoken word with small but still measurable loss. The other aspect of eighteenth-century recitative, the orchestrally accompanied variety, similarly evaded the problem. For while the practice of prefacing the best soliloquy arias with a dozen or so bars of *recitativo stromentato* produced passages of great beauty, often the most advanced and expressive musical style in the whole work, the result was far from the concise, narrative nature of genuine recitative, so far from being dramatic, in fact, as to stress the formality of the aria by separating it from the action, and acting as a buffer between the aria and the patter of *recitativo secco*.

Before *Orfeo*, Gluck makes little variation on the *recitativo secco* of the time. This style has been fully preserved in only one of the Milan operas, which, together with the arid expanses of it in the more mature works, gives us no reason to regret the loss. It was a curious convention in music, belonging exclusively to the Italian language and surviving in

serious opera only while the isolated aria had to be eased into the framework of the dramatic action. With both the diffusion of national opera
and the dethronement of the aria, it ceased to be either feasible or necessary. Gluck rejects it for the first time in *Orfeo*, though already in
L'Innocenza Giustificata Durazzo had taken a hand in speeding up the
drama by cutting down the length of the *secco* scenes. By the Paris operas,
it reappears fleetingly in the continuous texture of the action, alternating with and expanding into the more expressive *accompagnato* style. It is
the progress of the latter that can be most profitably traced through
Gluck's works: the metrical orchestrally accompanied recitative, the
first development which had liberated the Florentine recitative operas
from their self-chosen limitations. In the seventeenth century it evolved
to release composers from the unnatural lack of direction of their static
basic style. In the mid-eighteenth century it effected the same rescue
operation in the deserts of *recitativo secco*.

One unexpected fact emerges clearly from any study of Gluck's
accompanied recitative in the first ten operas – that each self-contained
passage is in emotional range and expressive technique as fine as anything Gluck wrote in later life. This is unexpected in that the early arias
made little attempt to scale the same heights. It is difficult to tell exactly
how conventional Gluck's accompanied recitative was. Certainly the
orchestral figures he uses and the harmonic vocabulary were a common
language throughout Europe wherever Italian opera flourished. It is
also fair to state that Gluck nowhere in these first works attempted an
extended scena in the manner of his greatest contemporary in this field,
Jommelli. Most of the *accompagnati* in these operas are inserted into the
normal flow of *secco* recitative and lead back into it, very much in the
early Baroque manner. A few passages occur immediately before an
aria. These last are the only occasions on which the key of the recitative
bears any relationship to the key of the formal music of the opera.

All the *accompagnati* in the Milan operas are for string accompaniment
– usually four-part: the richness of the harmony demands the independent participation of the viola far more frequently than in the arias.
There are three usual styles of accompaniment, all completely conventional since Handel, at least. The simplest form of accompaniment
serves merely to contrast the sustaining powers of the orchestra with the
ephemeral chords of the continuo which supports all *recitativo secco* –
hence the sustained chords and repeated patterns of quavers, usually
beginning on an up-beat unless a particularly unexpected accent is

required. The expressive effect arises purely out of the harmony, and the vocal line is more or less continuous above the changing chords.

The two other techniques are both more in the nature of interjections. Two figures were common, both in Gluck's recitative and in that of his contemporaries; the dotted rhythm, cascading up or down an arpeggio shape, and the rhythmic scale passage more frequently moving downwards. Often all three styles of accompaniment are found combined in an uneconomical richness of material that reflects every shade of 'affection' in the vocal line, with the prodigality of the immature artist. (EX. 19) The fact that orchestral figures interrupt the voice and break up the phrases of the text is of more importance than can be deduced merely from these early operas. It was later to be developed into one of Gluck's most powerful effects. The interpolative material then becomes more than conventional motifs, and expresses the emotions of the protagonists during dramatic pauses.

Not all Gluck's accompaniment textures are of such conventional shape, however, even at this stage. The recitative quoted above continues to range through a wide variety of styles, and this contrapuntal passage occurs towards the end of it. (EX. 20)

Because there was a limit to the normal accompaniment figures available, harmonic expression was the most individual aspect of these *accompagnati*. Gluck's vocabulary was surprisingly effective in comparison with the arias from this period, and the progressions he uses in these operas are essentially seventeenth-century. The frequent use of diminished seventh chords was a commonplace for increasing the tension, and for *en passant* climaxes. Gluck's harmonic language in the later operas changes, and relies less on these clichés. It is therefore all the more interesting to see how thoroughly steeped in the historically conventional Gluck was in his earliest operas. Tonics and dominants in various forms make up almost the whole vocabulary, and this range is emphasized by the limited vocal line, moving forward in a series of cadences. As in *secco* recitative, the vocal line is largely chordal, with auxiliary notes penultimate to the end of each phrase. It is compiled from a series of accepted formulae – the alternative cadences, for example, of the drop of a fourth on to the dominant, and the drop of a third (usually part of a *cambiata* decoration) on to the tonic. We have already commented on the continuous dominant-tonic progressions; this is the factor which drives recitative through so many keys, modulating, for example, to the subdominant key rather than resting on the subdominant chord.

EX. 19

It is obvious that this practice limits the vocal line to frequently recurring phrases – their recurrence giving shape to the otherwise direction-
less modulations – and limits it also to phrases of a cadential nature,
clinching the modulation. Any form of lyrical expansion of the vocal line
is precluded by this characteristic construction.

EX. 20

There are, however, moments of lyricism in the early operas that are
not by any means miniature arias, nor do they bear any relationship to
the recitative we have so far examined. This *arioso* style occurs once in
Ipermestra, and is placed, as with most of the *accompagnati* in that opera,
in the middle of a *secco* scene. (EX. 21). The singer, as in all the *accompagnati* in this opera, is Ipermestra. The accompaniment is for strings.
This style reappears in the later operas; Agamemnon's 'Diane impitoyable' and Orestes' 'Que ces regrets touchants' both use this expansion
of accompanied recitative, which, being both metrical and lyrical,
breaks all the traditional definitions of recitative and perhaps comes
closer to reinterpreting the intentions of the founders of opera than any
other musical style.

In the more mature operas, between the Italian apprenticeship and
reform mastery, we find Gluck gradually concerning himself more and
more with the problems of recitative. In the first operas there was no
problem. The styles existed, the libretto stood ready, and it is more
proper to respect the expressive variety Gluck produced in this limited
context than to criticize his lack of reformatory zeal in dealing with the
dull patches. From *L'Innocenza* onwards, however, Gluck found the
necessary change in circumstances to make recitative a problem to be
reckoned with. He composed more often original or newly edited

libretti, and the difference between these and the Metastasian pattern becomes increasingly obvious.

Durazzo wrote the recitatives for *L'Innocenza* and the immediately apparent result is their brevity – brevity of both the *secco* scenes and of

EX. 21

the meandering, introspective *accompagnati*. No great poetry is produced, but a number of small developments contribute to a greater realism and effectiveness. Durazzo's contribution probably showed Gluck, for the first time, the paramount importance of the librettist in constructing dramatic situations, for most of the dramatic situations in *L'Innocenza* occur in the recitative.

An important feature of both the *secco* and *accompagnato* recitatives in this and subsequent works is the increased use of dialogue – not the alternation of one long speech with another, but the short question and answer, comment and reaction returns of everyday speech, bringing accompanied recitative, hitherto reserved almost exclusively for the principal characters, among the ranks of confidants and minor characters for the first time. It must be remembered that any attempt to bring about a *rapprochement* between the gilded, artificial world of opera with its 'antique' code of manners and customs, and the contemporary life of the audiences who watched it, was a daring move. Opera had long flourished on an Aristotelian remoteness of protagonists, a Baroque intricacy of language, gesture and procedure. 'Noble simplicity', which Gluck attempts as early as this work, was not a quality guaranteed to be a success. Even the contemporary scenes of comic opera were remote – as remote from the lives of the courtly audiences as were the heroes of history and myth.

A new device for Gluck (though it had been used a number of times by Jommelli) in this opera is the placing of recitative to interrupt an aria, at the climax of the opera. (EX. 22). It is an obvious place for such a device, but this does not lessen the unexpectedness of its effect. The quickly changing colours as each modulation sweeps across the orchestra are the more vital after the restrained little G major aria with the unobtrusive pizzicato accompaniment.

A greater variety of accompaniment figures occurs in this opera. Gluck breaks away from the conventional interpolative rhythms for the first time. In the recitative 'Si, tene priego per tutto ciò', the continuous accompaniment of held chords and pizzicato arpeggios makes the fairly conventional vocal line sound almost lyrical. The orchestra also adds an *arioso* continuity of texture. Gluck becomes much more economical in his accompanying textures in these works, and a whole passage built up over one pattern, as in this example, is now the rule. On a bigger scale, this device can give a feeling of symphonic texture, and is an important contribution to continuous opera.

Another development in the middle operas is in the harmonic language, now much less dependent upon dominant and diminished sevenths. The unexpected chord-shift can be seen in this passage from *Telemacco*. (EX. 23). Although this work almost certainly post-dated *Orfeo* (the first available, but disputed, date is 1765), it has a number of characteristics of a pivot work, like *L'Innocenza*, and can be more conveniently illustrated here. It is the first work, apart from *Orfeo*, in which Gluck builds up continuous recitative-ensemble-chorus scenes: the 'interruption' in the last act of *L'Innocenza*, which was introduced because the situation required quite literally to be interrupted, has become in this opera a feature of Gluck's style – a style of continuity and flexibility which makes possible a number of passages of chorus writing

EX. 22

interspersed with recitative and solo airs, a fine omen for the chorus-soloist relationship in *Alceste* and *Iphigénie en Tauride*.

With *Orfeo* begins the splendid series of reform operas, each one far too individual a work to be dealt with in a general survey. In each opera Gluck faces anew the aria-recitative situation, and finds different solutions. In *Orfeo* itself it is immediately apparent that recitative was a foremost concern of the reform, for each of the acts uses it in a different way with a freedom of style and context that had not hitherto existed.

EX. 23

The recitative that interspaces the verses of Orpheus' song in the first scene plunges us straight back to the Baroque with the echo effects so dear to seventeenth-century composers:

EX. 24

Comparing this with the second recitative of the opera, we get some impression of the mounting tension throughout the scene: the stepwise vocal line includes wide, expressive leaps, and the harmonies become tenser, more dissonant. The first passage is in the tonic minor of the key of the song, and in the second recitative the tonic chord becomes a seventh chord resolving only in the sixth bar in the relative minor. The scene is designed to produce a cumulative effect of increasing power and freedom. The third recitative breaks into a new and violent style in the further removed key of G minor. This pattern of alternating song and recitative is most effective in these circumstances: the recitative is used in direct apposition to the aria in order to convey the extremes of emotion which would be out of place in the medium of song, the latter medium itself being a conscious act of characterization.

This extended movement leads into a scene between Orpheus and

Cupid, showing how Gluck uses *secco* recitative in the reformed works. It is hardly true to say he excludes it from *Orfeo*. The style as far as the vocal line is concerned is the same, but instead of the continuo unit, the whole string orchestra adds the punctuating chords. The presence of the orchestra has a number of advantages. The chords can be played with a far wider range of dynamics, and they can also be sustained. And a most useful innovation which results from the presence of the orchestra in scenes with more emotion than information is that the orchestra can expand into significance – and into true *accompagnato* style – without breaking the continuity. This free flow of styles is used extensively in the third act.

In *Orfeo* the considerable reduction in quantity of recitative is very apparent. Particularly in the second act Gluck manages Orpheus' entry into the underworld, for example, entirely through song and dance-chorus. The scena 'Che puro ciel' which follows this is somewhat in the manner of Jommelli's extended *accompagnati*, though for sheer beauty of physical sound it transcends anything the latter wrote. It is typical of the symphonic conception of opera that was to develop in the nineteenth century. The continuous texture of characteristic figures, rich orchestration and vocal comment, at times superimposed and elsewhere interpolative, come together to make up an entirely new style of *accompagnato* for Gluck: not a style that he ever returned to on so extended a scale, but enriching the already diverse vocabulary of recitative in this important and revolutionary opera.

In the third act, the main feature is the continuous dialogue. It is largely set out in recitative. As a drama, the last act fails because of a singular lack of cause and effect in its externals – insufficient reasons for Orpheus' provoking silence in the presence of his restored bride, and the amoral *deus ex machina* conclusion. Musically, it fails because it goes on too long. The duet, for example, is irrelevant, since it ends in exactly the same situation as that in which it started. The climax would have been far more effective had it not been anticipated many bars before. As it stands, the one really effective stroke is the sudden tension arising out of the momentary overlapping of voices. That the last act relies more heavily on its recitative than any other scene in the opera is not wholly coincidental with the dramatic failure of the act. Gluck was to develop his recitative style more powerfully as he pruned its appearances still more, and as it was combined more closely with the aria and chorus into a continuous and forward-moving whole.

The reversion to continuo-accompanied *secco* recitative in the Italian version of *Alceste* is the more surprising because this opera fulfils this aim of continuity more completely than *Orfeo*. There is very little recitative in the opera that is not incorporated in the continuous scenes. And again we find the wide variety of contexts. There are conventional *accompagnati* before Alcestis' big arias in Act I, and single dramatic strokes like the Oracle. There is also an aria (Admetus' 'Misero! e che faro') interrupted by recitative. The main innovation is the expressive interpolation of the orchestra, already mentioned. Instead of a stylized orchestral figure interrupting the voice, a self-contained melodic passage fills up the dramatic pause, expressing the emotions of the protagonists concerned. This happens, for example, in the third act of *Alceste* with the feature, that becomes characteristic, of the semitone-dropping harmonic progression:

EX. 25

In the revision of *Alceste* for Paris, all the *secco* recitative is scored for the orchestra, thus throwing doubt on the theory that Gluck reintroduced it because of rehearsal difficulties, since rehearsals were notoriously less satisfactory in Paris than in Vienna. Another interesting change is that the lyrical interpolation quoted above is removed from its context and used to introduce a short air by Evander, 'Nous ne pouvons trop répandre des larmes.' The subject is again Evander's tears, and 'oboe sighs' are added, as in *Iphigénie en Aulide*, but in spite of this colourful touch, by making explicit in the vocal *arioso* what had originally been merely implied by the orchestra, the dramatic effect of the passage is weakened, if not destroyed.

In *Paride ed Elena*, the recitative has a similar function to that in the first act of *Orfeo*. This similarity is to be expected between operas so closely connected in characterization techniques. The recitative expresses the violence of emotions that are otherwise clothed in the objective language of song. Wherever there are confidants, however, there will be dialogued recitative, where clarity of communication and contrast of character is more important than introspective monologue. After the smooth lyricism and small vocal intervals of much of this song-and-dance opera, scenes such as the fainting of Paris are both necessary and impressive. Particularly splendid in this passage is the revelation of the full character of Helen, from the imperious arpeggio dismissal of Erastus to the hesitant self-realization in the staccato orchestral phrase – another example of the dramatically necessary pause filled in by an orchestral expression of the character's emotional state, often revealing this more clearly than the words of the vocal line. (EX. 26)

With the Paris operas that now follow we have to consider whether Gluck's recitative was influenced by the native traditions of French opera to any marked degree. *Iphigénie en Aulide*, as we have already shown, is written in a very fluid style, shifting from informal air to accompanied recitative, to dance and chorus, with few full stops in either the music or the action. While this is a very French characteristic, it is also clearly the rational path of development open to Gluck, and without determining to what extent Gluck knew himself – and arranged his working life accordingly – it is impossible to distinguish external influences from personal preferences in the question of French opera. Certainly there are many pages in this opera that contain the rich variety of a page from Rameau – and provoked the Encyclopaedist-influenced audience to complain of lack of melody.

From a less-prejudiced point of view, however, it is difficult to see how Gluck could have combined lyricism, swift action, and intensely taut expression more effectively than in the scene where Clytemnestra and Iphigenia arrive; Calchas' warning of the inevitability of the sacrifice is fulfilled unexpectedly soon, and his recitative breaks into the weighty and ominously purposeful *misuré* phrase, 'Ils y trainent déjà ses pas'. Immediately the chorus enter for six excited bars, and the briefer accompanied recitative of Agamemnon ('Qu'entens-je? Juste ciel') follows, expressing nothing but complete bewilderment at the sudden reappearance of the danger he had hoped to have averted. This straggles into Calchas' air, with the superbly hymnic introduction, which for a short time reasserts the balance of formal music. Within twelve bars of the score, Gluck uses five different styles unified by the infinitely varied links of recitative. Gluck never ceased to make more

EX. 26

effective his actual harmonic progressions in accompanied recitative; thus Calchas' recitative that opens this fragment does not rest on a root position till it reaches the *misuré* style, where the rhythmic impetus carries it forward without the force of pending resolution of dissonance; Agamemnon's (conventional) diminished sevenths lie expressively between the simple chorus harmony and the hymn-like progressions of Calchas' aria.

Iphigénie en Aulide is probably Gluck's most strikingly orchestrated opera. There are few passages that express mood through instrumental colour as vividly as in Clytemnestra's anguished anticipation of her daughter's death, sinking to exhaustion at 'Ah, je succombe à ma douleur mortelle'. Gluck at this time would not have risked leaving the bassoon *sforzandos* and the oboe sighs undoubled by the strings, but it is the wind colour that predominates, and transforms what is melodically and harmonically one of the simplest passages into a memorable incident in the last act.

This figure we have called the oboe sigh becomes almost a mannerism in the later operas. It occurs in *Armide* when the vocal line refers to sighs and tears, 'Tu m'entends soupirer, tu vois couler mes pleurs . . .' This rather neglected opera contains more successful, continuous recitative than any other reform opera, succeeding, where the last act of *Orfeo* failed, to make complete scenes (the last two in the opera, for example) both musically interesting and dramatically effective. The large orchestra he uses contributes considerably to this. Gluck evokes evil and the supernatural as vividly with wind (oboe and bassoon) *sforzandos* as with the trombones in *Orfeo* and *Alceste*: Armida sings 'Mais après mon trépas ne crois pas éviter mon ombre obstinée à te suivre' to the accompaniment of angry semiquaver figures in the strings, and menacing held *sforzandos* in the wind – a particularly full texture for the low register of her voice at this point. Gluck adds clarinets to the wind section only in the final pages of the opera, where they rather indiscriminately double string scale-passages and sustain horn-like chords in their middle register. The oboe was Gluck's wind instrument *par excellence*, and a consideration of its qualities and characteristics reveals much of his dramatic art.

Armida, a colourful successor to Circe, is most fully characterized in the recitative. Her incipient madness is an obvious opportunity for wide leaps and unexpected harmonic progressions, especially contrasted with the tender Neapolitan harmony with its caressing semitones assigned to

Renaud in, for example, 'Trop malheureuse Armide'. A revealing scene is that in which Armida goes to kill the sleeping Renaud, the orchestra indicating her hesitation (in a phrase marked *lento e espressivo*) before she herself realizes it. This is a great opera, in spite of the less interesting scenes among the minor characters, with Armida dominating just as Alcestis does, and consequently dwarfing the rest of the cast. Apart from her large-scale traditional aria of conjuration, 'Venez, venez, Haine implacable', she makes all significant communications in recitative. This fact is as important and deliberate an aspect of characterization as the use of song in *Orfeo* and *Paride*. And the use of recitative was only possible because Gluck had developed it into such a rich and subtle language, fully effective for even the extended scenes of the last act.

Characterization through recitative is one of the many masterly techniques in *Iphigénie en Tauride*. This most continuously effective of all Gluck's operas contains no finer character-drawing than in the scenes between Pylades and Orestes. The contrast between the simple nobility of the man of action and the anguished fatality of the haunted contemplative is clearly set out in the opening scene of Act II. The orchestral opening, perfectly expressive of the silence and desolation of the scene, is a self-plagiarism from the ballet *Semiramide*, one of six such borrowings in the opera. The contrast between the two men is maintained, in words and music, throughout the scene. (EX. 27)

Another passage from *Semiramide* is used to fill the moment of pause where Iphigenia steels herself to sacrifice her brother. Again we find the semitone-dropping harmony and 'sighing' phrases Gluck uses so often in this context. The passage occurs at the beginning of a long and continuous scene of recitative, chorus, and brief passages of measured *arioso* that are a special development in this opera. The vocal line in recitative had for some time become less bound by traditional formulae, but the wholly lyrical passages like 'O mon frère', Orestes' 'Que ces regrets touchants', and 'Dans cet objet touchant' are closely connected with the short aria. Thoas' aria-fragment, 'De tes forfaits', leads into the climax ensemble, which is a very tense affair, carried out entirely in accompanied recitative. The hammering rhythms derived from 'De tes forfaits' build up tremendous tension and the various voices enter above it at arbitrary intervals. The climax itself is brought about by sheer physical action – the entry of Pylades and the stabbing of Thoas – and Gluck's success lies in his economy in this long recitative ensemble which creates suspense

EX. 27

Iphigénie en Tauride

by the very bareness of its melodic material and the elemental concentration on a simple rhythm.

Echo et Narcisse contributes nothing new to Gluck's recitative technique. It is mostly of the orchestrated *secco* type, with French and fanciful designations of zephyrs, sighs, and echoes.

Gluck's development of recitative can be seen, more clearly than in the case of aria, to be a continual expansion of the language. As the vocabulary grew it acquired new functions, and to attempt these before the idiom was perfected was the cause of the few failures. All that Gluck added to recitative was in the nature of a closer *rapprochement* with the style of the aria. To this end he freed the harmony from its Baroque enslavement to the diminished seventh, and created a much more melodic vocal line. The accompaniment accordingly grew in importance, till it was the rule to find it scored for full orchestra and constructed to hold the whole passage together in a texture full of individual character, and owing nothing to the limited patterns bequeathed by his predecessors. The emergence of the *arioso* was to be foreseen from each of these developments. Its appearance in Gluck's long recitative scenes provided a point of melodic expansion without slackening the pace of the drama. And drama is conveyed more effectively in the reform recitative than ever before in opera: dialogue is possible because the range of styles makes for clear-cut distinction between characters, and the economy of musical material leaves the physical action of the drama to speak for itself.

Gluck's development of recitative is possibly the most vital aspect of his reform of opera – vital in the sense that it lived into the nineteenth century, and developed in later works only along lines foreseeable from Gluck's own viewpoint. It is among his most original contributions to opera, owing a little to his librettists, but arising chiefly out of his very personal outlook on opera: it is necessary to be able to put drama before music before good recitative can be created.

Chapter six

Gluck's Development of the Chorus and Ensemble

The chorus very early became an essential component of Florentine opera. It does not appear in the earliest works of the Camerata, since these monodies were, far more than any of Gluck's operas, true 'reform' works, intended to destroy the choral tradition which had reached its highest point in the previous century. But in the operas of the more professional composers the chorus plays a substantial part from the first. Monteverdi's *Orfeo* (1607) is in no way limited by the theories of the Camerata; many of the choruses are in the madrigalian style which had been discarded by the theorists. In Monteverdi's operas the chorus has a similar function to the ritornello, that of giving form to the variety of short movements that make up each scene. This obviously arose because choral music was then still the norm that orchestral music has now become: the latter, in Monteverdi, generally either imitated the texture of the choral music or dealt in a primitive manner with a characteristic idiom of the instruments concerned, for example the fanfare 'toccata' of *Orfeo*.

The frequently contrapuntal ritornello choruses of operas from this period deteriorated rapidly with the development of public opera in Venice. It is difficult to see why this should have made so marked a difference unless the composers themselves were prepared to see the chorus disappear. The evolution is plain enough, however. In Monteverdian opera the singers in the chorus were at times necessary participants of the drama on stage, but when the chorus was fulfilling a purely interlude function they were quite simply in the way, and would have been better in the orchestra. When opera became popular, and the

economics concerned the reaction of the audience rather than the enter-
tainments budget of the ducal patron, many of the subtleties of form and
style were sacrificed to more immediately appreciated effects: thus the
splendid instrumental resources of *Orfeo* gave way to the simple string
orchestras of later seventeenth-century opera, the esoterically sensitive
language of monody was simplified into the more appealing aria and the
functional *secco* recitative, and the non-dramatic interludes of chorus and
ritornello were dropped completely. Where a crowd had an active part
there was a crowd indeed, but in such numbers that the management
could not afford to pay them all at singers' rates, and the music had to
be shortened and simplified so that these 'extras' could learn it. These
changes resulted in an opera that was in no way inferior to the first
operas – in many ways, indeed, it had more unity of style and more
dramatic effect – but it did result in the gradual rise of aria opera, the
lionizing of great singers, and the eventual all but total disappearance of
the chorus and the dance from each scattered outpost of Italian opera,
which together constituted the eighteenth-century musical world with
the single exception of France.

The chorus, dramatic in style though not in function (an important
distinction), was kept alive in the oratorio tradition. This, perhaps
strangely, had no effect on contemporary opera. Handel, for example,
has a very clear dividing line between the two genres, and any operatic
performances of his oratorios face the problem that Italy had faced in
the early seventeenth century.

In France the chorus was retained because opera had developed
along quite different lines. The indigenous art was the dance. Berlioz
wrote in 1834 that 'at the Opéra they would provide an excuse for a
ballet even in a representation of the Last Judgement'! With the ballet
entrées providing interludes in any case, the chorus soon became an
integral feature which French conservatism refused to uproot. Protected
by the Court patronage, French opera in its formative period never had
to adapt itself to popular demand, and rigidly repelled any attempts to
'modernize', develop or reform until the unsettling consequences of the
'querelle des bouffons' and the opening up of the famous stage to composers and styles of opera of international origin. It was very important
to Gluck (and to the composers who followed him) that the choral
tradition had been retained in this one country. Again and again we
have to turn to France as the only source from which his innovations
might originate, a source albeit more fruitful for the composers

of the Italian culture than for those to whom it was indigenous.

We have already shown the Italian tradition to be paramount in the first operas of Gluck. The use of the chorus in these may be taken as completely typical of the majority practice – always remembering that a few composers, notably Traetta and Jommelli, had discovered the French style and adapted it for their own use. None of the first ten operas, of Gluck's Milan period, boasts more than a *coro finale*. *Demofoonte* is one of the few for which we have the music: a lightweight movement in $\frac{3}{8}$ time. Throughout Gluck's life – with a very few exceptions, of which *Armide* is one – the last movement is considerably slighter in technique and emotional content than the preceding numbers. This practice corresponds with the suites, concertos, and symphonies of his contemporaries, which were invariably first-movement weighted. It is easy to condemn the finales of, for example, the two *Iphigénies* in the light of the nineteenth-century reversal of this convention. Gluck was never sufficiently far-sighted to foresee the specific possibilities of the ensemble finale in serious opera, and in spite of the development of his choral writing in all other contexts his closing movements remain the simple numbers (though often effective enough in performance) that appear in the Milan operas.

Occasionally there is no chorus at all. In these cases a tutti of soloists fulfils exactly the same function (as in *Ipermestra*, for example), although the need to write in the easily taught and easily learned style no longer exists.

Similarly there are few duets from this period; and only one trio, in *Ippolito*, of which the music is lost. The ensemble movement did not play an important part in the 'singers' opera' of this time. The growth of instrumental polyphony had had no lasting effect on the somewhat specialist ranks of opera composers. And the aria had been so exclusively cultivated that the ensemble style had no independent life, and followed the form and style of the aria as closely as possible. From the few examples in Gluck's Milan operas we can distinguish two different techniques of adapting the aria for performance by two voices: either alternate lines are sung by alternate voices, or the tune moves forward in parallel thirds and sixths. Gluck's duets combine these two techniques without deviating into more complex branches of counterpoint. There are no ensemble movements involving both chorus and soloists.

This wholly conservative use of the chorus and the ensemble persists far into Gluck's mature period. The first opera to use the chorus in a new manner is *L'Innocenza Giustificata*, a work which we have already seen to contain a number of innovations which reappear in the reform works. It is important to remember that Durazzo constructed the piece, and thus presumably dictated the role of the chorus. There are three full chorus movements. This in itself is a remarkable increase, but more significant is their placing: towards the end and climax of the drama. They provide Gluck with his first opportunity to portray the dangerous vacillation of a crowd – first demanding Claudia's death, and eventually acclaiming her innocence. The crowds in *Alceste* and *Aulide* are of the same type, though they are more fully drawn. Gluck's style is still somewhat formal and traditional in *L'Innocenza*, but he must have been aware of the dramatic effect achieved by the mere participation of the chorus after so long a sequence of arias, and this proved to be the starting-point for the development of a chorus style.

In addition to the three full choruses, the *coro finale* being taken complete from the fairly recent *Ezio*, Gluck (or Durazzo) also uses the effect of a chorus in a completely new way. The short interpolations of the 'semi-chorus' of soloists at the climax ('Ecco la nave al lido') gives exactly the same effect as the interpolations of the chorus of priestesses in a number of scenes in *Iphigénie en Tauride*. The device was not yet entrusted to the full chorus, but the technique, having been conceived, was to be of considerable further use.

Duets and trios from this period are still rare. In the last-mentioned example from *L'Innocenza* we can see that Gluck was prepared to treat a tutti of soloists as a small chorus. This had also occurred in the tutti finales of the earliest operas which had no chorus. So we may interpret as a new trend towards the ensemble finale the procedure in *Il Rè Pastore*, in which each act ends with an ensemble of varying complexity. The first act ends with a duet, 'Vannea regnar, ben mio'. This is certainly no advance in technique. It is of the same sort as the duets in the earlier operas – alternate lines, and occasional parallel passages for both voices. The second act closes with a quartet, one of the very few such movements in all Gluck's operas. Here again Gluck seems confined by the necessity to introduce all the voices and keep them going simultaneously, though he does extract a small amount of dramatic antiphonal effect. The possibilities for genuine ensemble writing are more or less excluded from the start by the distribution of voices in this opera: it was not uncommon to have four sopranos in important roles, but it was impolitic to designate the only two ensembles in the opera to combinations of these characters alone. The third act ends with the usual final chorus with which Gluck had also concluded his previous opera *Antigono*; it is a fine and vigorous tune and worth repeating, but the 'thin' treatment of it indicates how little time and energy Gluck apportioned to this section of an opera.

With the *opéras-comiques* Gluck begins to develop an ensemble technique for the first time. Hitherto, the duet, trio or quartet had received no independent style at his hands, being merely another aspect of either the aria or the chorus. But the sharp simplicity of this important group of French works left no room for an ambiguous purpose. Although most of the *trios dialogués* are based on the vaudeville 'form' of a series of tunes with no element of combined singing, some really vital duets can be found, arising from the fresh, lively characterization of these operas. The second duet in *Le Cadi Dupé*, for example ('Qu'en dîtes-vous, Monseigneur'), between Zelmire and the Cadi, uses contrasting styles for the two singers to a far greater extent than in the Italian operas to date, and the dialogued method shows off this contrast with some realism, though the action obviously proceeds more slowly than when the singing is simultaneous. From this plurality of characterized styles, the more contrapuntal duets emerge naturally. An excellent example of these is the movement (which later becomes a trio) 'Maudit Ivrogne' from Act I of *L'Ivrogne Corrigé*, in which actual simultaneous singing does not predominate, but the swift exchanges between the characters and the good bass line give the impression of continuous three-part movement. *L'Ivrogne* is one of the few comic operas that has a proper chorus. A quartet of soloists takes this part in most of the smaller works, in *La Fausse Esclave*, and *L'Arbre Enchanté*, for example. *La Cythère Assiegée* uses both chorus and dance. But *L'Ivrogne* is the only one to use the chorus to create an extended and continuous scene; the mock fury scene which occupies most of the second act was the longest Gluck had written up to this time, and the music is especially noteworthy for successfully conveying the sometimes genuinely serious mood in a style always consistent with that of the rest of the opera. In fact, although there is no continuous movement involving soloists and chorus, the alternation of Pluton and his pair of furies with the hymn-like choral music gives the impression of a much larger structure than Gluck actually creates. *L'Ivrogne* stands immediately before *Orfeo* in the creation of such vivid ensemble tableaux.

Before the reform, then, Gluck rarely ventured outside the conventional in his use of the chorus. And the conventional consisted of the minimum usage involved in a final chorus. *L'Innocenza* contains the only hint of a freer use. The ensemble was in the same subsidiary position, occurring more frequently than the chorus but having even less independence of style. Not till the *opéras-comiques* did Gluck experiment with a dramatic approach to the duet and trio. In the reform operas both chorus and ensemble become immediately more important. In only two reform operas (*Paride* and *Armide*) does the chorus play anything other than a dominant role. It is naturally to Gluck's librettists that we owe the physical presence of the chorus in these scores; but the evolution of a most versatile chorus style, a style already masterly in *Orfeo* and infinitely flexible and varied in the Paris operas, can be credited to Gluck alone.

It is surprising that the chorus is not specifically discussed in the *Alceste* preface. Compared with aria and recitative the changes it undergoes in the reform works are drastic, and can only be attributed to the most indirect influence of other composers. They can be shown, however, to derive from two of the avowed aims in the preface: the diminished prominence of the arias focused attention for the first time on what went in between; and in the creation of 'varied spectacle', that Gluck attributes to Calzabigi, the presence on stage of a chorus and ballet became desirable.

These two circumstances caused at least two different styles of chorus to emerge. The most striking 'spectacles' in Calzabigi's operas are what we have called the tableaux scenes: Orpheus and his mourners around the tomb of Eurydice, Paris and his train at the altar of Venus. They are usually attributed to Calzabigi's French tastes, but it is important to remember that Rameau had written very little on the scale of these movements, and that Gluck can scarcely have known any of his music intimately. There is, of course, nothing in Italian opera of this epoch to approach this style. When Gluck expands these scenes into the one-movement solo and chorus tableaux of the Paris operas – the opening prayer scene and the later funeral rites for Orestes from *Iphigénie en Tauride*, for example – he is closer to mid-seventeenth-century opera than to any contemporary technique. The other choruses take place in the recitative scenes into which Gluck aimed to incorporate arias with something approaching complete continuity. The choruses play a substantial part in achieving this continuity. They vary from a few chords to fairly extended comment or ejaculation; the development of this aspect of chorus writing runs parallel with Gluck's development of recitative and *arioso*, being elementary in *Orfeo*, but sustaining almost the whole action in the *Iphigénies*.

Gluck's development of the chorus, then, is tantamount to the creation of a new idiom for opera. To a far lesser extent than in the reform of aria and recitative does he build upon the already existing foundations of *opera seria*. It is because of this considerable originality of approach that Gluck's work in this field is so interesting. The chorus was obviously of the greatest significance to the reform, and Gluck's revitalizing of it results in some of the finest choral scenes in the history of opera.

We must now discuss some of the actual choruses in the reform operas. These can be examined in four categories according to their function in the drama. First – because Gluck first developed this type and because it recurs throughout the reform operas – is the chorus we have already described as belonging to a scene of spectacle, where half its impact lies in the visual effect. These scenes require of the singers a variety of style which had not hitherto been needed: a complete and massive tranquillity is the only manner in which to perform the opening choruses of *Orfeo*; but in the equally devotional prayer scene at the beginning of *Iphigénie en Tauride* the music requires a more impassioned performance, and this is perhaps one of the choruses that Gluck had to teach the Paris cast to act. A further variety arises when dance is combined with the chorus. Of all the operas, *Iphigénie en Tauride* maintains the closest relationship between the ballet *entrées* and the plot, and as a result it is the opera to introduce dancing characters most successfully. The Scythians in the first act and the furies in the second are completely relevant because of the continuously potent characterization in both choruses and dances. We can see the same effect aimed at but failing in *Paride ed Elena*, where the dances of the Spartans are splendid in their own way and full of personality, but the same characteristics applied to the sung chorus fail to achieve so original an effect, and we are presented not with one chorus character, but with two. The unanimity of style between the Scythian chorus 'Il nous faillait du sang' and the three subsequent ballet movements is quite complete.

An important part of the visual effect of these scenes would be played by the costumes of the chorus. We have unfortunately no complete account of these, and though the practice was to display superb examples of seventeenth- and eighteenth-century fashion, a movement had started in France towards greater realism of costume. The Opéra had long been famous for the elaboration of its costume. For a revival of *Dardanus* in 1763, 'les habits même du choeur étaient ornés de pierreries ce que l'on n'avait jamais vu'. Noverre was instrumental in destroying this tradition, but as early as 1734 a production of Rameau's *Pygmalion* had been given in London, creating a sensation verging on the scandalous by the simple Grecian costume of the heroine. In Paris the first step towards realism in costume seems to have been in the 1760s, and then the most daring of concessions was the rejection of 'paniers', so we can hardly expect Gluck's characterization of the barbaric and the supernatural to have received much assistance from the appearance of his cast. The composer Laujon put on his opera *Sylvie* in 1766 with such improvements as most sensitive composers were trying to obtain at this time: 'j'exigeai, je dirai plus, j'obtins d'abord la suppression des masques . . . l'introduction des costumes nécessaires à tous les personnages, sans excepter la danse et les choeurs. Antérieurement à cette époque les choeurs arrivaient sur la scène en marche réglée; les hommes d'un côté, les femmes de l'autre . . . chantant, les hommes les bras croisés, et les femmes un éventail à la main, tous enfin ne se permettre aucun geste.'

The function of these chorus scenes in the reform operas was invariably that of establishing a mood or atmosphere. This is why they tend to occur at the beginning of acts and indeed of whole operas. The deeply serious and tragic tone of 'Ah se intorno' is necessary before Orpheus can translate the same emotions into the artist's grief, in the major-key songs. *Iphigénie* begins on a note of physical turbulence illustrating in the most obvious terms the mental torments that are to follow for all the protagonists in the drama.

A second type of chorus is predominant in two of the reform operas not yet discussed. This is the active chorus, in which the singers take part in the physical action on stage, and it plays a most important part in both *Alceste* and *Iphigénie en Aulide*. Gluck's portrayal of a crowd in both these operas is masterly, and his correspondence and reported conversation show that he had thought with originality on the subject. Corancez, although described as 'un véritable ignorant en musique', was instrumental in introducing Gluck to Rousseau. Corancez describes many of his visits to Gluck, and the latter's patient and ingenious replies to his questions. To his criticisms of the monotony and unstriking quality of the soldiers' choruses in *Iphigénie en Aulide* Gluck is reported to have given the following answer:

'Ces soldats . . . ont quitté ce qu'ils ont de plus chers, leur patrie, leurs femmes, et leurs enfants, dans la seule espérance du pillage du Troye. . . . Supposez . . . qu'une province étendue éprouve une forte disette. Les citoyens, en grand nombre, se rassemblent et vont trouver le chef de la province, qui se présente à eux sur le balcon: – Mes enfants, que demandez-vous? Tous répondront à la fois, Du pain! – Mais est-ce ainsi que vous devez. . . . Du pain! – Mes amis, on va pouvoir. . . . Du pain! Du pain! A toutes les observations ils répondront Du pain!; non seulement ils ne prononceront que ce mot laconique, mais ils le diront toujours du même ton, attendu que les grandes passions n'ont qu'un accent. Ici les soldats demandent la victime; toutes les circonstances sont nulles à leurs yeux; ils ne voient que Troye ou le retour de leur patrie; ils ne doivent proférer que les mêmes mots et toujour avec le même accent. J'aurais pû sans doute faire un plus beau choix musical . . . mais je n'aurais été que musicien, et je serais sorti de la nature que je ne dois jamais abandonner.'

It is the sheer irrelevance of the bustling, inflexible demand 'Nommez-nous la victime!' that contrasts so dramatically with Agamemnon's agonizing situation. Gluck paints an easily stirred crowd: genuine excitement is the only emotion expressed in the brief, unexpected outburst 'Clytemnestre et sa fille', and there is a whole-hearted, if not sentimental, admiration in the graceful chorus 'Que d'attraits, que de majesté'. In *Alceste* the crowd is represented more sympathetically. There is a splendid nobility in the opening 'Ah, di questo afflitto regno'.

These choruses are all short compared with the extended movements previously discussed. They put forward the people as a collective protagonist essential to the drama. It is not surprising, then, to find them chiefly in the operas which concern the relationship between a king and his nation. It is for a people capable of the spontaneously tender exclamation 'Misero Admeto! Povera Alceste!' that Admetus must accept a death for his own life. And the anger of the apparently insensitive crowd at Aulis is necessary to bring Agamemnon to the point of agreeing to the sacrifice. In spite of the vivid humanity with which Gluck and his librettists endowed them, Alcestis and Iphigenia are seen as mere possessions of their kings, in contrast with the vital relationship between their husband and father respectively, and their nations.

Very close to these active choruses are the even briefer fragments

Gluck interpolates in the recitative scenes, occurring almost exclusively in *Iphigénie en Tauride*, though the furies' 'No!' in the second act of *Orfeo* is in the same category. Here, the effect is highly realistic, and the spontaneity of the interjection is the most necessary quality to achieve in performance. The shortest example is probably the priestesses' single chord on 'Ciel!' when Orestes reveals the murderer of his father. In the last act of *Iphigénie* they have more short entries, brought about by the particularly close relationship between themselves and Iphigenia, so that every crisis of emotion she feels affects them also.

EX. 28

Gluck's choruses, then, are not merely an arbitrary aspect of the operas. They are invariably most convincingly motivated, and are essential to the full portrayal of the principal characters, since it is so often on the relationship between the principals and the chorus that the drama depends. For this reason a fourth category of chorus is important, although it somewhat overlaps the first (scenic choruses) in function. It is, however, a new technique when a soloist is combined with the chorus in a continuous scene or movement, whether the singing is antiphonal or simultaneous.

The best example is the finale to the second act of *Iphigénie en Tauride*. Here Iphigenia and her priestesses perform the burial rites for Orestes, whom they believe dead. It is an extended movement, allowing in the orchestral ritornelli for a certain amount of 'business'. It makes a suitable concluding movement for the first half of the opera, by balancing the first movement of the first act. And we have already seen Gluck tending towards the idea of an ensemble finale. The material is not new. The main theme first appeared as the middle section to a famous aria from *La Clemenza*, of which the outer part reappears as 'O malheureuse Iphigénie' in this opera; it had also been used as 'Que de grâces' in *Iphigénie en Aulide*. It is very nearly unique among Gluck's great tunes in being essentially contrapuntal in conception:

EX. 29

Gluck proceeds to use it on a simple chorus-air-chorus basis. The subtleties lie solely in the orchestration (the tragic colouring of funereal flutes, and supernatural trombones), and the scheme of tonality which alternates major and minor versions of the tune on the tonics of C and E flat.

Not all Gluck's combinations of soloist and chorus are as straightforward or as unified as this. Orpheus' scene with the furies at the beginning of the second act of *Orfeo* is in the same category, but the movement is chopped up by the self-contained units of air and chorus. Nevertheless the unity of the whole scene is present in the continuous material of the choruses, which Gluck makes continuous by the very simple device of repeating the original rhythmic pattern. There are no other movements on this scale, but the many small air-plus-chorus numbers in, for example, *Alceste* and *Armide*, serve to underline this trend of vastly increased participation for the chorus.

The technique of chorus writing employed by Gluck is basically two-fold: the homophonic and often hymn-like effect of the processional choruses, and the contrapuntal texture usually associated with the briefer 'action' choruses. In the choruses of the first type – often, as a result of Gluck's choice of subjects, actual 'liturgical' hymns – we are made very aware of the fact that Gluck aimed at a simple effect and did not waste unnecessary complexities of part writing where they would not be heard. This is the style of all the final choruses from, presumably, *Artaserse* to *Echo et Narcisse*. The individual parts are dull and unmelodic. The effect is usually massive and splendid. An interesting departure from this practice is the unison chorus which ends *Iphigénie en Aulide*. The unison singing suggests a certain spontaneity which is lacking in the fully scored finale to the second *Iphigénie*, for example. For this reason it would have been possible to attribute the unison to a desire for realism, had not Gluck shown with an abundance of examples that realism, like rationality, was the last quality he was interested in incorporating in an operatic finale. In the course of an opera, however, unison was a powerful weapon for Gluck, as we see in the fury chorus 'Chi mai dell' Erebo', where simplicity and dramatic effect illustrate the main qualities of his reformed style.

The homophonic style, however, occurs in a number of contexts other than the *coro finale*. Gluck uses it invariably for any movement that is even slightly formal – such as the welcome of Clytemnestra and Iphigenia to Aulis, the hymn to Venus on the shores of Sparta, the melancholy choral opening of *Alceste* – where his aim is to establish a certain mood. This he readily achieves by the broad hymnic style, relying chiefly on the harmonic colouring to define the emotion expressed. (EX. 30) Gluck also uses this style for any short chorus where sudden unanimity of feeling is an important dramatic point: the 'Piangi, O Patria', again from *Alceste*, and, from *Iphigénie*, the sudden horrified calm which overcomes both the soloists and the chorus after the quickly moving denouement of the fate of the house of Agamemnon. (EX. 31)

Gluck's contrapuntal ability is a much-maligned aspect of his technique. The truth lies in the fact that it was as irrelevant to his conception
of opera as it had been to the musical language of the early symphonists.
Caldara was the last composer to work in the elaborate seventeenth-

EX. 30

X. 31

century style. Jommelli attempted complex textures in his ritornelli, but
abandoned them in the more dramatic parts of his operas. Rousseau's
'return to nature' supported rather than promoted his era's desire for
simplicity in art. Gluck was wholly typical of his contemporaries in his
artistic aims, but suffered an unnecessary amount of criticism both
because he was the first composer to attempt such aims in the field of
Italian *opera seria*, and because his apparent musical abilities indicated
that the style resulting from these aims was perhaps no more than a *pis
aller*.

Gluck, however, successfully uses a contrapuntal texture for a very
few dramatic situations where its effect is obviously most carefully
chosen to carry out a certain dramatic function. It occurs almost
exclusively in the choruses of action – and usually only in those conveying particularly vigorous action, if not confusion. Two choruses of
horrified flight, for example, occur in *Alceste* (in the first act, after the
pronouncement of the Oracle) and in *Iphigénie en Aulide* (Act III, 'Fuyons

tous; d'Achille craignons le courroux'). In these movements the contrapuntal texture plays an important part in portraying the confused
agitation and surprise of the chorus, particularly after the ceremonial
hymnic style which has closely preceded it on both occasions.

A very different kind of counterpoint is found in the furies' chorus
'Vengeons et la nature' in *Iphigénie en Tauride*, where the chorus sings
more or less homophonically and the counterpoints are added chiefly by
the orchestra – at first in the conventional 'running bass' and later in the
little tags of Fux-like polyphony in the upper orchestral parts. The effect
again is of movement, and also of a variety of tensions, appropriate to
the scene of retribution. Gluck's dramatic use of counterpoint in
choruses can scarcely be surpassed. There is not time, in the fast-moving
drama of these reform operas, for a movement of any length in the
circumstances Gluck chooses for this device. There is not time to expose
any deficiencies of technique. The whole effect is achieved by the fleet-
ing view of chaos among the ordered progress of the rest of the opera.

Contrapuntal choruses appear only very rarely in the earlier operas.
There were, of course, none of the short movements to which Gluck
usually assigns this technique. The two solemn and fairly extended
choruses in *Telemacco* are interesting exceptions. 'Quai tristi gemiti', in
the first act, is a most impressive movement in the style of a Rameau
mourning scene. There is nothing very complex in the contrapuntal
style; it is 'open' counterpoint, so that rarely more than two voices are
singing simultaneously, but the device is unusual for Gluck. The movement that follows this provides the material for Agamemnon's opening
prayer in the first *Iphigénie*. It appears first as an aria for Telemachus,
and is taken up by the chorus in a curious 'octave' disposition of parts –
basses and contraltos answered by sopranos and tenors. These are among
the few genuinely contrapuntal moments in Gluck's choruses. As we
have said, it was for him a style assigned to a specific dramatic purpose,
and its freer use would have been a fault against characterization.

The ensemble movements in the reform occur much less frequently
than the choruses. Because they never acquired a distinctive genre or
form in the pre-reform operas, they tended to decline as the aria
declined, their dialogue function was taken over in the new and more
substantial recitative and the mere appeal of euphony in art had been
rejected. Duets and trios in the reform operas tend to fall into two
groups: those with a semichorus effect, where the actual appearance of
an ensemble movement at that point in the music seems to be more

important than the substance of the libretto; and the essentially 'dialogued' numbers where the contrast of personalities and purposes is the
sole cause of the music.

The semichorus ensembles are usually weak in dramatic effect and
contribute little or nothing to the characterization. *Iphigénie en Aulide* is
unfortunately full of these ineffectual movements; the second act
quartet (to which the chorus is later added) 'Jamais à tes autels', has no
conflict between the participants, one of whom is the supremely uninteresting Patroclus, and it achieves nothing that could not have been done
by a group of soloists from the chorus. This is surely a weakness in any
ensemble, for it is a denial of the powerfully built up characterization
that is apparent whenever these characters sing alone. The third act
finale contains two ensembles where this style is rather less out of place,
'Mon coeur ne saurait contenir' and 'Les dieux ont eu pitié', since the
universal relief and rejoicing is the dominant mood of the whole scene.
Generally, however, the appearance of a quartet in the score gives rise
to these completely undramatic numbers, whose only justification lies in
the contrast of texture and pace which marks them off from their contexts.

Gluck wrote a few excellent duets and trios in the reform operas.
These occur only where the characters involved are important enough
to be contrasted vigorously with each other, and where the situation
convincingly gives rise to simultaneous singing. Ensembles of this intensity were certainly unfashionable both in Italy and in France. De la
Harpe, one of the most prolific contributors to the journalistic controversies that surrounded Gluck in Paris, wrote: 'J'avais observé, (à
propos d'Achille et d'Agamemnon) qu'il n'est nullement convenable à
la dignité de deux Héros de parler tous les deux ensemble, comme dans
les querelles du vulgaire.' Gluck's successful ensembles are, in fact, an
aspect of his fidelity to nature, an extension of the realism he brought to
recitative by therein introducing dialogue, and to aria by the rejection
of the symphonic ritornello.

The most interesting trio is probably 'Je pourrais du tyran,' from the
second *Iphigénie*. In effect it is more of a duet, Iphigenia offering life and
release to one of her captives, and Pylades and Orestes unanimously
claiming it for the other. It is a very short movement, with three varied
strophes of the solo tune answered by the duet, and then a much freer
ending in which Iphigenia makes the choice she has already long since
made. The movement dissolves into recitative at Orestes' anguish on

hearing that he is to be spared. This is closely followed by the duet between Orestes and Pylades, 'Et tu prétends encore que tu m'aimes?' This is a most spontaneous movement, springing out of the recitative without a single chord of introduction, and proceeding from dialogue to the impasse of mutual desire to be Iphigenia's victim.

EX. 32

The dramatic power of this movement alone is a testimony to the superiority of Pylades over the long line of confidants from which he has sprung. We are early in the opera aware that he is a hero in his own right: 'Que peut la mort sur l'âme des héros? Ne suis-je plus Pylade?' and this is a necessary preliminary to such a duet as this in which he

plays a part equal to Orestes' in self-sacrifice and love. The two characters are well distinguished in the music – Orestes habitually despairing,
bitter, almost savage, and Pylades alternating between tenderness and
his characteristically rather melodramatic brand of heroism.

Gluck thrived on such conflict and drama. The duets between his
lovers, throughout the reform operas, are undistinguished musically.
The younger Iphigenia never comes to life with her Achilles as completely as she does in the later opera with her brother. Paris and Helen
become a very mundane pair when they are finally reconciled. Orpheus
and Eurydice are never sufficiently established as human characters in
the earlier parts of the opera (Orpheus represents simply an apotheosis
of grief in song; Eurydice makes scarcely any impression as a woman)
for their duet scene to be other than a disappointment after the superb
preceding acts. Alcestis and Armida both so heavily outweigh their
counterparts in sheer power of personality as to make any duet including
them unbalanced. In fact, the responsibility for successful ensembles lies
in no small part with the librettist. Gluck's collaborators rarely provided
him with the opportunity to repeat his successes.

With both the ensembles and the choruses it is apparent that all
Gluck's significant developments occur after the turning-point of the
reform. The ensemble was not important to him and it was more by
chance than design that the few excellent examples of it came into being.
The chorus interested Gluck profoundly. It is the most strikingly
'reformed' aspect of *Orfeo*, and was developed to be a dramatic force as
potent as any of the principal roles by the late Paris operas. It is, moreover, one of the most individual developments of the reform, and, more
clearly than any of the innovations in aria and recitative, led the way
towards the creation of an international style, the 'music for all nations'
that Gluck had looked forward to at the beginning of the Paris operas.

Chapter seven

Gluck's Development of the Overture

GLUCK's development of the overture is the one aspect of his work that begins only with the reform. In fact, it is not until the second reform opera that any indication of development can be seen. The Italian opera overture had long fallen into insignificance in the opera house; though the number of early eighteenth-century overtures that were published and performed in instrumental concerts indicates that the composers tended to take them more seriously than the audiences. Nine untitled overtures by Gluck survive, possibly dating from his earliest period, for of the first ten operas, only one, *Ipermestra*, retains its overture.

The three-movement structure, originating in Naples, was the accepted norm at the beginning of the century, and Gluck used it intermittently as late as *Paride ed Elena* and the two *opéras-comiques* he revised for Paris. Deriving from the concerto, it maintained the characteristic bifurcation of tutti and solo material. The overture was substantially weakened when the chordal, non-melodic tutti style was adopted as the predominant texture outside the concerto context that justified it. It is this style that is represented in the *Orfeo* overture and that seems both irrelevant and unsubstantial beside the rest of that opera. Its irrelevance is perhaps no greater than that of the contrived ending to this and to all tragic operas of this era. Gluck soon learned to write tragic overtures, but only *Armide* of the reform operas has its conclusion brought about by the actual chain of events of the drama.

The negligible material of the unreformed overtures arises solely from the widespread use of what was originally a texture, as a subject. It has one justifying quality, something we shall call 'overture mood', which is present in all great operatic overtures, and the misunderstanding of which led Beethoven through such difficulties in providing a fit prelude to *Fidelio*. This mood has something in common with the fanfare with which the earliest Florentine operas were introduced. There is the immediately communicable atmosphere of excitement, and the very absence of any significant musical substance tends to draw the listener on to more important things. In *Orfeo* (and *L'Innocenza* and *La Clemenza* and *Ezio*, etc.) the drama begins with the rise of the curtain; in *Alceste* it begins with the first notes of the overture; in *Iphigénie en Tauride* the drama and the overture both begin with the rise of the curtain: thus we may condense Gluck's development of the overture, to trace which we have little enough material, but decisive progress at every stage.

In the *Alceste* preface Gluck requires that his overtures shall not only introduce the mood of the opera, but also set forth its argument. Berlioz points out the impossibility of the latter claim: 'The overture to *Alceste* may announce scenes of desolation and tenderness; but it cannot reveal the object of the tenderness or the cause of the desolation. It can never tell the audience that Alcestis' husband is a king of Thessalia, condemned by the gods to lose his life unless someone offers to die in his stead. . . .' Nevertheless, the material of the reform overtures is often based on characteristic music – and music that Gluck increasingly associates with specific characters or incidents in the course of the opera. The *Alceste* overture is the 'purest' in this sense, devoid of any but the most tentative and ambiguous reappearances in the opera. But it was the first overture to introduce so unequivocally a tragic action.

Like all Gluck's instrumental music, it is simply constructed, being in a very clear-cut binary form, the second half merely repeating the first half in the dominant key. It is not completely continuous with the first scene, which opens with the herald's trumpet call, but it ends on the dominant chord, thus leaving 'open ends' to lead easily into the action. In style it has surprising affinities with the earlier overtures. It opens, indeed, with the most solemn arpeggio phrase and proceeds to the tender, tragic oboe theme; but contains also string passages of unmelodic material similar to the concerto tutti patterns that comprise most of the *Orfeo* overture. These passages, which one critic has called 'sawdust', are, in fact, important to preserve the 'overture mood' of the piece. It is not a symphonic poem on the subject of the opera: it is a movement designed to prepare, to excite and to usher in the drama that is to follow.

The melodic material, like the form, is very simple. The opening arpeggio is the only figure that can be said to recur in the opera. But with so commonplace a motif it is difficult to be certain that the connexion was anywhere intended. Two examples will clarify this: the temple scene in the first act positively bristles with similar arpeggios, and as this figure is the chief unifying factor in the scene we may take it to be significant, and chosen deliberately; the odd figures that are later tossed into Admetus' recitative 'Lasciatemi crudeli, in van sperate' are surely only conventional *accompagnato* tags. Gluck could have made this association with the overture much clearer had he intended it to be noticed. The contrast of tutti and solo textures of the original overtures can usually be found in Gluck: after the impressive opening for the full orchestra, the string section gradually leads into the next tutti with a fairly contrapuntal passage based entirely on Gluck's characteristic sighing phrases.

Apart from the trombones, Gluck has only a small orchestra (two each of flutes, oboes, bassoons, and horns, plus strings) which he uses with no particular style. The individual qualities of the woodwind are often, Schubert-wise, plainly denied, as in the beautifully expressive second subject, where flutes and oboes double each other throughout. There is very little feeling of the brass as a section, the trombones being present more as a stage property than as an extension of the normal orchestra. This convention of certain instrumental combinations having fixed characteristic qualities was a potent influence on mid-eighteenth-century orchestration. The 'Turkish march' colouring, which persists as late as the finale of Beethoven's choral symphony, was inevitably for Viennese composers as real a legacy of the Turkish wars as were the coffee houses and Oriental fashions in furniture and entertainment. At the other end of the scale the idioms of Bohemian dance music coloured symphonic dance movements by Haydn and his contemporaries long before any intimations of the 'folk' movement were discernible. For the overture to *Paride ed Elena* Gluck selects a very common but none the less characteristic instrumentation – the martial trumpet and drum combination, immediately conveying an atmosphere far from the supernatural mood of *Alceste*.

This is the last of Gluck's serious overtures to be cast in the old three-movement form. There is a reason for this choice, for the *raison d'être* of the opera lies in the contrasts of characters and nations, contrasts so sharply drawn that the two styles cannot comfortably appear within one

movement. In presenting this duality of musical language Gluck goes
farther in presenting the argument of the opera than he did in *Alceste* –
still with the limitation that he cannot convey events in music – since
this opera has so few incidents and so much static affirmation of the con-
flicting characters.

The first movement of the overture is the march the scoring suggests.
It divides clearly into two halves: the first, an alternation of tutti and
episode passages linked by the strong rhythm of the opening phrase and
the syncopation that occurs in each of the episodes; the second half is
more continuous in texture, having the 'overture mood' we mentioned
in *Alceste*, with a striking arpeggio phrase in the bass that later returns in
the opera for the appearance of Pallas Athene, providing the orchestral
material for her accompanied recitative. The march leads straight into
the second movement – for strings only, *con espressione*. This is a very brief
glimpse of the soft Phrygian mood of Paris's music, the tune is throughout 'softened' by the two-note phrases and anticipations that colour
Paris's songs in the first and third acts:

EX. 33

Paride ed Elena

This is followed by the closing movement, in which the main tune of the
march is transformed into a lyrical dance in $\frac{3}{8}$. The first act opens with
the hymn to Venus which is continuous with this, in mood and metre;
so that although the overture comes to a rather more finished cadence
than the *Alceste* overture, it has an even more definite feeling of leading
into the opening scene. The second and third movements both reappear
in the penultimate scene of the opera; the slow movement as an interlude for the orchestra alone and the $\frac{3}{8}$ dance as a brief duet, 'L'amo,
l'adoro', in this rather piecemeal ensemble.

Gluck could have attached no importance to this re-use of material at this stage. It was probably prompted by motives of convenience, no more significant than those that permitted the revival of material from earlier operas. As a deliberate device, the use of overture material in the course of an opera is in any case of doubtful value: for, as the overture is heard first, it is meaningless on its first appearance, and while its repetition might arouse a vague awareness by the audience that the moment is especially important, neither the dramatic nor the musical effect is necessarily enhanced. The worst product of this practice was the pot-pourri overture that became common in the nineteenth century, serving no greater artistic purpose than the street corner hurdygurdies that Meyerbeer hired to popularize the tunes from *Les Huguenots* before the first performance; the best result was the growing unity of style that we first become aware of in *Iphigénie en Aulide*, which undoubtedly attracted Wagner to this work, and prompted his anachronistic revision of it.

Iphigénie en Aulide is the best of the reform overtures. All the tendencies that had begun to appear in *Alceste* and *Paride* here assert themselves as part of the whole dramatic plan of the opera. Musically it is the most distinguished overture. And it was not surpassed: for *Armide*, Gluck unaccountably – and how many of his disappointing moves are completely unaccountable – revived the old-style overture from *Telemacco*. In the second *Iphigénie* he is attempting a different problem, at once more dramatic and less musical in its import. The overture to *Echo* is one of the finest things in the opera, but still it does not approach for sheer interest, relevance, and attractiveness the superb prelude to the first of the Paris operas.

The similarity between the form of this overture and the traditional French one must be coincidental. Gluck would have selected the andante from *Telemacco* for the opening had it been performed in Vienna, Rome or London. Moreover, the andante designation of the opening is nowhere contradicted in the second, 'fast' movement; and this often accounts for a clumsy speeding up half-way through, in performance – since the first unison phrase of the 'fast' movement needs quite as steady a speed as the introduction, yet the bustling 'overture mood' must be retained among the very nearly continuous semiquaver movement.

In *Telemacco* the introductory material appears as an air-plus-chorus, always uncompromisingly set out in the bare three-part writing that is so effective in this quiet beginning. The orchestration in the overture is interesting. Gluck, as usual, avoids a genuine antiphony between instrumental groups; it is not 'strings: wind' but 'strings: strings-plus-wind'. The use of bassoon and viola as the bass instruments gives a clarity rarely heard in Gluck's orchestral music. If one did not know of the pre-existence of this material one would be tempted to write at length on the nobility of the rising fifth and measured rhythm of the first phrase; the tension (semitone dissonance) to which this quality is subjected; and the tender, regretful sighs of the second phrase, indicating the intimate nature of the catastrophe. As it is, one had better keep quiet! But the fact is unchanged, that Gluck could not have found more appropriate music to reveal the basic emotions, and almost the basic situation, had he composed it afresh for the occasion, and the genius that decreed this quiet, almost breathless opening to the drama must be of the very highest order.

The main movement of the overture retains, as we have said, the genuine mood of expectation proper to the atmosphere of any theatrical entertainment. It is characteristic music – more so than in many of Gluck's fast overture movements – and much dramatic point is made of the antiphony between registers: the essentially lower-strings first theme and the alternately upper-strings and woodwind subsidiary themes. It contains one of Gluck's rare independent oboe passages: (EX. 34) – the 'cri plaintif de la nature' that reappears so consistently throughout this opera, originating in the second phrase of the introduction to the overture, and recurring, among many other instances, towards the end of Act II, the conclusion of Agamemnon's scene beginning 'Tu décides son sort'. (EX. 35)

The progress towards one of Gluck's aims – to link the overture more continuously with the first scene – can be traced through each overture in the reform. *Iphigénie en Aulide* is the first to have complete continuity with the music of the opera: immediately after the 'third time round' of the unison theme it breaks off and leads straight into 'Diane impitoyable', both rounding off the overture and re-evoking the atmosphere of beginning. In *Iphigénie en Tauride* Gluck goes the whole way and opens his first scene with a dramatic prelude: 'la pièce commence avec le premier coup d'archet.' In doing this, he suddenly took a step forward into a new artistic (and social) world, for the opera without an overture presupposes an audience ready to give it their serious attention from the first note; in fact, Gluck holds back from plunging us immediately into

EX. 34

Iphigénie en Aulide

EX. 35

the middle of the action by prefacing the storm with the brief 'calm'
scene. And the storm begins only quietly.

It is very much a tone poem rather than a formal movement. The
string figures come from the descriptive prelude to *L'Isle de Merlin*, but
the working out, and working up, of them is quite new. The orchestra is
a large but not a characteristic one, like those used in *Alceste* and *Paride*:

piccolo and flutes, clarinets, oboes, bassoons, horns and trumpets, drums, and strings – by far the biggest orchestra Gluck had used, and he produces a fuller sound with it, with more independent passages for the various woodwind instruments. For the first time in his instrumental music there is a consistent use of brass, wind, and strings as potentially self-contained sections. The piccolo, which comes into its own later in the barbaric music of the Scythians (Gluck's recurring concern with characteristic racial music), enters for the first time with the rain and hail where it is necessary to reinforce the flutes in their independent melodic line above the whole orchestra. The clarinets have few solo passages until the final dying down of the storm where the now harmless scale passages trickle through the orchestra. (EX. 36). The introduction of both the solo voice of Iphigenia and the chorus of her priestesses gives a simple strophic frame to the movement, and increases the resources of colour, with the very high tessitura of the solo line and the much less brilliant responses of the chorus.

True to the overture function already established, this movement presents a mood and an emotion rather than conveys events. We are not to know, and indeed the point is never specifically made, that this is the storm that brings Pylades and Orestes to the Scythian shore. It has the 'open ends' of the earlier *Iphigénie* overture and as the storm subsides it leads very skilfully into the passage of recitative with which the action continues.

Any aspect of *Echo et Narcisse* poses a problem, but the overture is perhaps the least problematic, since it contains all the maturity of style, the full textures and new colours of the best music of the opera, without the monotony that palls long before the ending of the last act. Gluck uses a small range of instruments, but deploys them in an unusual combination which, as we might expect from his previous reform overtures, has the purpose of illuminating a certain aspect of the drama; in this case the relationship between the double orchestra texture and the intrinsic natures of both Echo and Narcissus is obvious. The two orchestras are used antiphonally throughout, and are unequally composed, the first and most continuously playing containing pairs of oboes and horns and a full string ensemble, and the second orchestra having the much less substantial forces of pairs of clarinets and bassoons, and two violin parts only.

The form is a free sort of binary again, with a wide range of moods from the gracefully pastoral to the deeply expressive. (EX. 37)

EX. 37

In its self-contained form this overture is a definite retrogression from *Iphigénie en Tauride*, but this is the baffling point that makes the whole opera difficult to accept in a chronological account of Gluck's development: that it contains some of his most beautiful music is irrelevant to a discussion of his qualities as a dramatist. It best testifies to Gluck's lively and experimental attitude to opera even in his sixties: the attitude that caused him to accept the commission of five companion operas to *Iphigénie en Aulide*, and that would perhaps have produced another complete opera at least, had not the failure of *Echo et Narcisse* been so complete and so discouraging.

Gluck's reform overtures reflect very clearly the continuous evolution of his reform style and his initially stated aim. Their influence on succeeding opera was profound. What Gluck achieved was no less than the creation of the overture as part of the drama; and in the development of descriptive orchestral music that resulted from this lies in no small measure his contribution to the new conception of the symphonic poem.

Chapter eight

Gluck as Dramatist

THROUGHOUT its history opera has attracted only a small proportion of composers to devote themselves to its exclusive claims – few composers have never written an opera, fewer still have written virtually nothing else – but it is among this small number of specializing composers that the most significant names in opera are found.

Gluck, however, is unique even among these specialists. He is remembered, revived, criticized, and appreciated not as an opera composer alone, but in an even more finely segregated category as a dramatist and dramatic reformer of opera. In this one field would appear to lie his whole pretensions to interest, let alone merit. And Gluck himself was chiefly responsible for this. He endeavoured 'to forget he was a musician', sought to compose 'in accordance with Nature rather than in the interests of musical variety', and whether, in fact, he sat down to compose with these principles before him or not, he so publicized his attitude to operatic composition that we are bound to accept his intention even if we doubt his consistency in practice. We have followed the musical developments he brought about in each of the important spheres of opera, and have tried to show the reform in the context of the sympathetic climate of thought of the age. It now remains to assess Gluck's achievement simply as a creator of drama in music, to isolate his qualities as a dramatist from his technique as a musician; and to examine in detail the finest drama he constructed, *Iphigénie en Tauride*.

In basing our examination on one opera rather than on a survey of his development, it is intended to give a clearer account of Gluck's dramatic methods and also a more complete impression of his music in context than has previously been possible. *Iphigénie* is undoubtedly Gluck's greatest opera. On the strength of this one work he is lifted out of the category of pioneers and established as a successful composer. In musical style it is the most consistent opera that he wrote since the earliest Italian period; and dramatically it is unfailingly effective.

Many of the qualities that determine the dramatic effectiveness of an opera are present in the libretto, and the choice of poem is an aspect of composition that was becoming increasingly important in Gluck's lifetime. There are two accounts of Gluck's choice of Guillard's libretto for *Iphigénie*. The more attractive is given only in Brissot's *Mémoires*: Brissot describes the young and impressionable Guillard (he was twenty-seven) writing the poem in a white-hot fever of admiration for *Iphigénie en Aulide*. The first two acts were taken to Du Roullet and when Guillard returned to receive his criticism he was carried off in secret to Gluck's residence, where Gluck at once sat down and played the young poet the music of the entire first act. The more widely traditional story tells that Gluck hesitated to accept the libretto for some months, suspecting a second *Roland* affair with Piccinni,[1] and only when Grétry expressed interest in the libretto did he finally decide to set it himself. In the event it was Piccinni who was deceived, since he had been offered the subject but accepted it only on the understanding that his setting should be given first – which it was not. The most certain facts that emerge are Guillard's intense admiration for the earlier *Iphigénie* and the influence of Du Roullet on his work. There are many parallels between the operas, but in most cases Guillard's poem achieves distinction where Du Roullet's was merely effective. It is a remarkable work for so inexperienced a writer.

Guillard's source was Euripides. It was perhaps sheer luck that his material existed already in a form so much more satisfactory than the Aulis legend. The necessity for Agamemnon's sacrifice of his daughter seems remote and uncompelling beside the more comprehensible threats of Thoas. The Iphigenia/Achilles relationship is a diversion from the essential action of the earlier story, while nothing in the events at Tauris is distracting from the main theme. Strikingly different are the parts played in the drama by the two interventions of Diana. In Aulis she

---

[1] 'When I discovered that the directors of the Opéra, who knew well that I was composing *Roland*, had given this very work to M. Piccinni to compose, I burnt as much of mine as I had finished. . . .' Gluck to Du Roullet, published in the *Année Littéraire* in 1777.

seems wilful, illogical, and her action as unjustifiable as the festive ending to *Orfeo*. In Tauris, which drama is, of course, only brought about by a negation of the Aulis ending, her appearance is on the one hand necessary as the only swift solution to the confusion of the scene of Thoas' death; and on the other it brings about no sudden reversal of the progress of events already set in motion, but merely confirms and makes smoother the Grecian victory over the Scythians, and the dissolution of Iphigenia's bonds.

Guillard, then, started with a good plot, and his exposition of it is wholly appropriate. Much of Du Roullet's methods can be seen in the actual layout of the opera, but *Iphigénie en Tauride* is a more modern work than *Iphigénie en Aulide*: there are more Italian-style arias, but their placing is more inevitable; there is more lyrical recitative than in *Aulide*; and fewer of the essentially French short airs. Briefly, *Tauride* is a more international opera, and is limited by fewer traditions, both in the libretto and in the music, than any previous opera in the reform. Some characteristics of the libretto were to reappear in nineteenth-century opera in all its diversity of national and international styles; those which occur in *Iphigénie* and which differ from Italian opera are threefold: first, the construction of many scenes round the active participation of the chorus. Gluck had already expanded the Italian practice beyond recognition in *Orfeo*, but not until the Paris operas did the chorus play so active a role dramatically as well as a musically important one. Then, in *Iphigénie*, for the first time the motivation of the ballet was satisfactorily solved. This was ever to be a danger point on the French stage, and Grand Opera tended to return to the abuses of early eighteenth-century works. For Gluck, however, *Iphigénie en Tauride* is the first opera he had written in which it would be unthinkable to cut the ballet sequences; short as they are, they are necessary to restore the balance of non-vocal music to Italian opera, and in their brevity to restore dramatic relevance to French opera. We have said that the recitative in *Iphigénie* represents an important advance. Guillard's contribution was to construct, even more than Du Roullet had done, dialogued scenes incorporating both action and reflection. Gluck's superb transformation of this material into significant music is among the strongest workings of his dramatic genius.

The poetry of the libretto measures up to the music on almost every occasion. There are some splendid lines for Thoas in particular, expressing the baffled, superstition-ridden barbarian:

Je ne sais quelle voix crie au fond de mon coeur,
Tremble, ton supplice s'apprête!
La nuit de ces tourments redouble encore l'horreur,
Et les foudres d'un Dieu vengeur semble suspendus sur ma tête!

in contrast with Orestes – equally menaced, but understanding his fate –

Dieux! qui me poursuivez, Dieux! auteurs de mes crimes,
De l'enfer sous mes pas entrouvrez les abîmes,
Ses supplices pour moi seront encore trop doux!
J'ai trahi l'amitié, j'ai trahi la nature,
Des plus noirs attentats j'ai comblé la mesure.
Dieux! frappez le coupable, et justifiez-vous!

For the chorus there are strong rhythms which Gluck seizes on to
powerful effect:

– Vengeons le sang de notre Roi!
– Grands Dieux, sauvez son frère!

And apart from a slight emphasis of the courtly manner in Pylades'
character, which is reflected occasionally in his words, there are no
deviations from the simple clarity of the language of the poem.

One last feature of the material Gluck chose to set that must be considered is the very rich cumulation of irony that exists in the Greek
original and is re-created most faithfully by Guillard and Gluck. The
very storm with which the opera opens is merely a physical manifesta-
tion of Iphigenia's antipathy to her enforced bondage as priestess:

Le calme reparaît, mais au fond de mon coeur,
Hélas, l'orage habite encore!

Her dream – drawn by Gluck in most powerful recitative – of the fate of
her family, piles horror upon horror with a vivid nightmare quality culminating in her enforced 'sacrifice' of Orestes. Much of the tension in
the first half of the opera is built up by such prophetic images of the
events which become real in the second half. In the second half the
drama lies in the actual incident. Thoas' prediction of his own death at
the hands of any strangers allowed to survive in his land is not only

terrifying, it is true. Other ironical incidents are merely fantastic in their impact: the funeral rites performed for the living Orestes, and the appearance of the shade of Clytemnestra which fades into the real entrance of Iphigenia to deceive the tormented Orestes. Gluck's contribution to this important aspect of the drama lies in the contrasted moods he evokes for the two pairs of acts. Most of what occurs before the end of Act II is dominated by the sustained threat hanging over Iphigenia and the fatalistic acceptance of his persecution by Orestes, both represented in the music by quiet tensions: the pianissimo chorus 'O songe affreux! Nuit effroyable!' and the prolonged pause which follows Orestes' declaration to Iphigenia of his own death, '[Oreste] a rencontré la mort qu'il a longtemps cherchée; Electre dans Mycène est seule demeurée.' Compare with these passages the sheer energy of the music of the third and fourth acts – the duet for Pylades and Orestes, the purposeful hymns of the priestesses, and Iphigenia's stormy grand aria 'Je t'implore et je tremble'. Gluck does not fail to interpret the mood in all its subtleties in this pregnant libretto, the potentialities of which are fully realized in his powerful setting.

We have said that *Iphigénie* is Gluck's most international opera. The full integration of the many styles he had used up to this point results in the rich variety of language in which he unfolds the drama. Gluck's choice of musical style is central to his achievement as a dramatist, particularly in setting a libretto which gives him such freedom in this respect. His main musical contribution to opera is the continuity which enables the pace of the sung drama to approach more closely that of the spoken script. Both this intention and the means by which Gluck accomplished it are symptomatic of his era, with its loosening of formalism in art to the end of finding a more natural, at times even a more realistic, truth. The dramatic ideals of eighteenth-century Italian opera, in so far as they existed, were concerned with the single movements from which the opera was built. Gluck's ideals were directly opposed to this. In interesting himself in the linking of the single movements he was bound to some extent to destroy the forms of those movements; we have seen in particular his development of the 'open-ended' overture. He did no less for aria and chorus, and, still consistent with his ideal of continuous drama, his use of a continuously interesting recitative lies at the heart of his achievements as a dramatist.

Gluck's use of traditional, closed forms is virtually limited in *Iphigénie* to moments when the drama contains ritual or ceremonial action: the two prayer arias of Iphigenia, 'O toi qui prolongeas mes jours' and 'Je t' implore, et je tremble'; and the hymns 'Chaste fille de Latone' and 'O Diane, sois nous propice'. Gluck can use these movements to convey formality only because of the absence of such forms in the remainder of the opera. His other use of the straightforward *da capo* form occurs in Pylades' aria, 'Ah, mon ami, j'implore ta pitié', where the absolutely clear-cut simplicity of the form is used to make a point of contrast with Orestes' madness, and disjointedly accompanied recitative, in the preceding passage.

The remainder of the opera, however, is not written exclusively in a recitative-based style. Gluck makes vivid dramatic use of movements which begin conventionally enough – that is, as if they are to become completed movements – and are interrupted both by incident on the stage and by the less formal style of recitative or ensemble. Two examples of this show the tremendous effect of the suddenly broken off movement which has already got firmly under way as a self-contained unit. Both interrupted pieces are incidentally remarkable for the vigour of their rhythm. One occurs at the end of the fury chorus 'Vengeons et la nature'; the prevailing contrapuntal style has given way to massive unison rhythms in the chorus, with Orestes' cries of a few notes irregularly across the phrases –

EX. 38

G.O.–H

A second example occurs in the last act; Thoas enters to disrupt the happy reunion of Iphigenia and Orestes, and breaks into what appears to be the first section of a full-scale aria. It modulates, as if to start the middle section, and just as Thoas is in full swing with a repeated note phrase ('Que tout son sang expie . . .') Iphigenia interrupts him ('Qu'oses-tu proposer, barbare!'), and so begins the ensemble of conflict which passes through momentary pauses at the revelation of Orestes' identity, and Thoas' death, only to end finally at the appearance of Diana.

Further usage of self-contained movements in the opera is restricted to variously shortened arias: the binary form arias which are, in fact, *da capo* arias without the reprise – Pylades' 'Divinité des grandes âmes', which suggests at the beginning a far more expansive setting for this act finale than Gluck allows himself to carry out. The same form appears in the earlier aria 'Unis dès la plus tendre enfance'; Gluck seems consciously to avoid portraying Pylades on a bigger scale than his small part in the drama requires, and yet succeeds in endowing him with the dignity that his role as Orestes' friend demands. Other arias are self-contained in form, but not in style; both Thoas' 'De noirs pressentiments' and Iphigenia's 'D'une image, hélas' have the irregular rhythms of recitative and, particularly in the first instance, the most casual and subservient orchestral accompaniment that gives the aria the informality of *arioso*, of which Gluck makes frequent and original use in this opera.

EX. 39

Apart from the arias and choruses mentioned, Gluck sets almost all the remaining poem in recitative. The power and variety he had at his command in this medium are indicated in every bar. Gluck makes use of three distinct styles of accompanied recitative in this opera: the lyrical *arioso* into which the shorter arias nearly merge, the dramatic and very fully orchestrated passages largely associated with the visitations of the furies, and the quickly moving narrative recitative in which most of the dialogue is carried out. This range of styles had been available since the beginnings of opera, but not since the earliest seventeenth-century period had composers availed themselves of it for so extensive a proportion of their operas. Gluck's employment of it was obviously dictated by his ideal of continuity, and was immediately appreciated by his critics: 'Il n'y a qu'un beau morceau – c'est l'opéra entier.'

Gluck's use of *arioso* is very close to that of the earliest opera composers. Most of the *arioso* is given to Orestes, which contributes to the drama in that Orestes' character is not sufficiently ordered to be expressed in the formal language of aria. And so we have the famous 'Le calme rentre dans mon coeur' and the intensely beautiful 'Que ces regrets touchants', both revealing Orestes' thoughts with an intimacy that he is not sufficiently controlled to conceal. In the last act Gluck uses the surprising effect of *arioso*, illustrating the advantages of his dramatic method over a more predictable Italian setting; immediately after the mutual recognition of Iphigenia and Orestes, Iphigenia breaks into the short phrase

EX. 40

O mon frè - - re, O mon cher O - res - - te!

which has the effect of lyrical relief after the tension of the previous action, and yet scarcely interrupts the pace of the denouement. Passages like this amply justify Gluck's principles of the function of musical beauty in opera: their effectiveness lies partly in their brevity and rare occurrence and partly in their dramatic truth.

The accompanied recitatives, melodramatic rather than dramatic, that are associated with Orestes' madness are rather more conventional. Handel or Jommelli would have done the same. Gluck scores them for full woodwind and trombones, making, perhaps, the distinction between horn and trombone colour that arises in the two statements of the *grave et marqué* passage in Act II, scene 3. The trombones are only used for the actual presence of the furies in the *ballet pantomime de terreur*; the horns are used instead when Orestes tries in vain to invoke them: 'Dieux! Protecteurs de ces affreux rivages, Dieux! avides de sang, tonnez!'

The bulk of the recitative is, however, accompanied by the strings only, being of the type we earlier described as 'orchestrated *secco*', but more readily expandable into *arioso*, with more varied accompanying rhythms, harmonic colouring, and interposed orchestral phrases than any previously found in Gluck. One of the most important scenes in this recitative style is that in which Iphigenia questions Orestes about his past and her family. Gluck builds up the scene by gradually increasing the participation of the orchestra and the urgency of the harmony; the accompaniment expands from a single ♪♩ figure in each bar, through more sustained chords, tremulo accompaniment, the addition to the orchestra of a single chord from the chorus, and finally the 'accompaniment' takes over the whole expression in two orchestral passages which appear after the two most horrifying revelations to express the overwhelming emotions of Iphigenia and her priestesses more effectively than they could in words. It is in the handling of such scenes that Gluck's dramatic skill has its fullest scope, independent of the structures prepared by the librettist and of the conventions of form of his age. The dialogues between Pylades and Orestes have already been cited as containing some of Gluck's best recitative. Again, the appeal of these scenes lies in the natural alternation of climax and anticlimax, the strongly differentiated characters, and the realism of pace re-created in the music.

Gluck's stylistic variety, then, both in its range and its appropriate selection, is one of the surest indications of his genius as a dramatist. Another aspect of his contribution to the drama may be seen in his use of colour – vocal and orchestral. Gluck had in the *Alceste* preface expressed his intention to handle the orchestral instruments 'in accordance with the interest and intensity of the words'. In *Iphigénie* he has the largest orchestral forces at his disposal. The extra instruments – piccolo and trombones – are limited to the contexts in which they are traditionally characteristic, the barbaric and the supernatural respectively. But in his use of the more normal wind instruments Gluck finds a freedom that was quite new to him. The full scoring of much of the recitative was, of course, only another aspect of the continuity of the opera. But Gluck does also choose his instruments to give a greater impact to the words, as we see in the accompanied recitative of Iphigenia's dream, at the beginning of the first act: the oboe is always closely associated with a 'speaking' quality, either the voice of conscience or of actual speech, in Gluck's operas. He scores the dream passage for string accompaniment throughout with scattered woodwind entries – oboes and flutes together in chords – the first of which occurs at the line 'Du milieu des débris fumants sort une voix plaintive et tendre', and another at the words 'On me crie, Arrête! C'est Oreste!' The only other use of the wind in the whole passage is the momentary reinforcement of a fortissimo climax when Iphigenia sees the murderous phantom of her mother. Gluck's dramatic illustration of the voices of first Agamemnon and then Orestes is simply but strikingly achieved.

Gluck's use of the oboe is always interesting and he rarely fails to give his most eloquent solos to this instrument – the long vocal melody in 'O malheureuse Iphigénie' for example; and where only one upper wood-wind instrument is added, as in 'Je t'implore et je tremble' and Diana's *accompagnato*, it is almost invariably the oboe that he uses to balance the voice. He does not make much independent use of the flute for dramatic reasons. It has one prominent passage, Orestes' *arioso* 'Que ces regrets touchants', where its peculiarly funereal and death-invoking qualities are of paramount dramatic impact. The clarinets are used extensively. Gluck isolates their rather thick and solemn tone quality for the sacri-ficial hymn 'Chaste fille de Latone', and for the chorus the priestesses sing when they believe Orestes dead, 'Patrie infortunée'.

This is one chorus in which Gluck attempts something in the way of consciously planned vocal colour: the second sopranos take the upper part at the highest point so that a feeling of tension is achieved without rising above the small and subdued compass of the melody. It is a striking example of the composer's range of expression that in this darkly coloured chorus movement he conveys the same utter despair and desolation that are transformed in the following movement into the limpid, poignant G major of 'O malheureuse Iphigénie'. On the whole the choruses are connected very closely in terms of colour with the arias of the principal characters with whom they are associated. The priest-esses even take over the function of confidant to Iphigenia, and this dramatic role is the chief reason for the numerous solo plus chorus movements they share with her. The Scythian choruses are harshly coloured, not only by the percussion band and shrill woodwind, but by the use of two very high tenor lines and a fairly high bass.

The essential power of any drama lies in the strength of the charac-terization. For incidents, however sensational, are of little lasting interest if the people to whom they happen are feebly conceived or ineffectively drawn. We have discussed Gluck's developing powers of characterization at frequent points earlier in this study, and it only remains to point out his sure handling of the characters in *Iphigénie*. *Opera seria* always suffers in comparison with comic opera in this respect. Its characters almost invariably belong to a long tradition of sung and spoken drama, and possess already an incipient dignity which severely limits the introduction of any idiosyncratic characterization. Pylades can exclaim, 'Am I not Pylades? Art thou no more Orestes?' and in any country where classical culture is traditional half the dramatist's work is done for him. In eighteenth-century France this was certainly true, and Gluck's aim was to identify these famous protagonists with music that was not inappropriate, rather than to create his characters from pure invention. In this he succeeds far more in the second *Iphigénie* than in the first. The only reason, apart from his developing ability, seems to be the unconventional condition of the characters in Guillard's poem. It was remarked in one of the earliest notices of the opera that the word 'love' was not uttered during the course of the whole four acts, and this freedom from the bane of eighteenth-century Italian opera, the inescapable duets between lovers that prove to be the weakest point in *Orfeo*, *Paride*, and *Aulide*, together with the equality of dramatic status of each of the participating characters – the absence of confidants and the close involvement of the chorus – gave Gluck a drama already exclusive of dramatic weakness to which his setting added only strength.

Gluck's dramatic genius has overshadowed appreciation of his purely musical developments in opera. He is the first composer of whom this can be said, and the fact is perhaps more indicative of the directions in which opera was to develop than specific to Gluck's own character. He was not the first composer to distinguish between music descriptive of action and music designed to accompany action, but he was the first composer whose talents and inclinations equipped him to adopt a certain approach to opera simultaneous with an external movement towards the same dramatic ends. Gluck's position in the history of opera is paradoxical. His influence on his immediate contemporaries was insufficient to found a school or create a style of opera even for the duration of his own lifetime. His impact on history lies wholly in the extra-musical achievements of his career – the idea of Gluck's reform was essential to Berlioz, Wagner, and most subsequent operatic composers, without the musical facts of the reform operas being more than indistinctly known to any of them.

Gluck as reformer has had all the renown he could have hoped for: as musician he has been almost totally neglected. A just appreciation, however, can only come about by a reversal of this situation; the qualities that made the first performance of *Orfeo* an historic occasion can never be recaptured by generations for whom *opera seria* is but one of many systems of opera, and an unfamiliar system at that. But the music of Gluck's greatest operas remains dramatically true for all eras, and can be re-created for those to whom the history of the reform is unknown.

Bibliography

Algarotti, Francesco, *Saggio sopra l'opera in musica*, 1755.

Berlioz, Hector, *Gluck and his operas*, trans. Evans, 1914.

Burney, Charles, *The Present State of Music in France and Italy*, 1771. *The Present State of Music in Germany, the Netherlands, and United Provinces*, 1773.

Calzabigi, Ranieri, *Dissertazione su le poesie drammatiche del sig. Abate Pietro Metastasio*.

Casanova, Giacomo, *Mémoires*.

Cooper, Martin, *Gluck*, 1935.

Desnoiresterres, Gustave, *Gluck et Piccinni*, 1872.

Einstein, Alfred, *Gluck*, trans. Blom, 1936.

Gluck, C. W., *Alceste*, Preface, 1769. *Paride ed Elena*, Preface, 1770.

Grétry, A. E. M., *Mémoires*, 1789.

Grimm, F. W. von, *Le Petit Prophète de Boehmisch-Broda* (satirical pamphlet), 1753.

Kurth, Ernst, *Die Jugendopern Glucks* (Studien zur Musikwissenschaft), 1913.

Leblond, Gaspard, *Mémoires pour servir à l'histoire de la révolution opérée dans la musique par M. Gluck*, 1781.

Marcello, Benedetto, *Il teatro alla moda*, c. 1720.

Masson, Paul-Marie, *L'Opéra de Rameau*, 1930.

Newman, Ernest, *Gluck and the Opera*, 1895.

Noverre, J. G., *Lettre sur la danse*, 1760.

Rousseau, J. J., *Lettre sur la musique française*, 1753.

Tiersot, Julien, *Gluck*, 1910.

Tovey, Donald F., 'Gluck', in *The Heritage of Music*, ed. Foss, 1934.

Wotquenne, Alfred, Thematic catalogue of Gluck's works, 1904.

Index of Gluck's Operas and Ballets

FIRST PERFORMED

General Index

The Collected Correspondence
and Papers of
CHRISTOPH WILLIBALD
GLUCK

EDITED BY
H. and E. H. MUELLER VON ASOW

'The most comprehensive collection of documents relating to Gluck ever published.'
Music and Letters
'The personality of the mature Gluck is vividly revealed . . . the richness of character that emerges is fascinating.'
Times Literary Supplement
'It is a privilege to meet him, in both his strength and his weakness, and in the context of his world.'
WILFRID MELLERS, *The Guardian*
'We must be particularly thankful for this chance to study the man as well as the musician.'
Musical Opinion

Medium 8vo, 15 plates
30s

BARRIE & ROCKLIFF
LONDON